PLAYING The Odds

Eternity's Your Bet

by JAY CARTY

VISION™ HOUSE PUBLISHING, INC.

Gresham, Oregon

TABLE OF CONTENTS

IS YOUR HOUSE ON FIRE?

(Somebody loves you a lot.)

Assume you are my neighbor. It's three in the morning.

You see smoke coming from my roof. Or maybe it's from the chimney? You think . . . *Is that a fire? I'm not sure. Jay is inside asleep. Should I wake him? If it's just the chimney he might get mad. I think I'll play it safe and go back to bed without telling him . . . I sure don't want to risk making him mad. Besides, it's probably only the chimney.*

How would I feel toward you if my house burned to the ground? How would I feel if my house was on fire and you were afraid to tell me? Would I feel neighborly? Close? Hardly! If that's the depth of our commitment, I don't have much of a neighbor in you, do I?

Some neighbors would take the next step by calling the fire department. That's more than the first guy did and it would make them somewhat better neighbors.

But the fella' I want living next door is the one who would call the fire department and then dash across the lawn in his "tight whites," throwing himself against the front door, hurting his shoulder when he discovered it was dead bolted. But this guy wouldn't give up. He would then hurl himself through the plate glass window into my living room. All cut up and dripping blood on my white wool carpet, he would then thunder up the stairs to my bedroom yelling, "Jay, get up! Your house is on fire! Your house is on fire!"

If it was only the chimney, would I be mad?

Probably—at least at first. But after thinking about it I'd realize I could fix the dent in the door, replace the plate glass window, and clean the carpet. But where in the world could I find another neighbor who cares that much about me?

Did someone give you this book? The uncaring thing for that person to do would have been to hope your house wouldn't burn while fearing it would—to not risk waking you up. The someone who gave you this book may have been calling the fire department on your behalf by praying, and that's good. And that person, who must really care about you, didn't stop there. He or she put your relationship on the line. This friend cares enough about you to want you to spend your eternity in paradise, not in torment.

Now, you may think there is no hell. You may not believe there is a God. Or you may think you've been good enough to get to heaven on your own. But I hope you'll respect your friend's passion enough to consider the odds on what he or she believes to be correct . . . because, like it or not, there is a choice to be made—a bet to be laid.

With this choice you want the best odds you can get. With your soul on the line and eternity to spend, this is too important to be wagering on a long shot, especially when you consider the upside potential and the downside risk.

CHOCOLATES AND CHOOSING

(Forrest Gump was only half right.)

"Life is like a box of chocolates," Forrest Gump said to anyone who sat on his bench. "You never know what you're going to get."

Sometimes you win big and sometimes you lose big.

A young woman won big when she was chosen to be the first schoolteacher to participate in the space program. But she lost big shortly after blast off. Was she lucky, or unlucky, or both? Wasn't being in the federal building in Oklahoma City when the car bomb exploded bad luck? Weren't those who were supposed to be in there, but weren't, lucky? I don't know.

Life's a lottery, some say.

My Grandma Hattie said it from a different perspective as I stood with my arm around her at the grave site. She had outlived her daughter. "We'll take what the Lord gives and like it." Now that's a different twist. Forrest Gump tells us life is a matter of luck. Grandma Hattie said God is in charge.

I honestly don't know who is right. Forrest or Grandma Hattie, or both? How much of life is luck (God backing away and just allowing "things" to happen and letting the results of sin to run their course) and how much of it is governed by his sovereignty?

Don't expect me to have the answer; I'm an old athlete, not a philosopher or a theologian. Besides, volumes have already been written about life and nobody has come up with good answers to those questions, so I won't try. I just want to remind you . . . there are some events in life over which you have absolutely no control. You not only reap what you sow, you also have to take what you get. No choice.

But eternity is a different matter entirely. Until the moment of your death, you can live it up. You don't have to take the first chocolate you choose, eat it all in one bite and slam it down the hatch. But the risk—if you choose to delay—is that you can't predict the moment life will end. You can't be sure, with each split second it can take for a life to end, that the eighteen-wheeler doesn't cross over into your lane, that the nutty chocolate caramel doesn't lodge in your throat with noone but Fido at home to give you the Heimlich, that your worst nightmare doesn't whisk you into eternity unprepared.

If our souls last forever (the odds affirm that probability) then living eternally isn't a choice. You can't opt out of forever. But *where* you spend eternity is your choice. Life only lasts a life-time and you have to take what it dishes out. Eternity, on the other hand lasts forever, and you can do something about it.

I want to help you make an informed decision about what you will do with your life after death. It's the most important decision you will ever make. In the pages that follow I'll share with you what I know about eternity. But more importantly, I'll tell you what your choices are.

Get ready to make your choice by placing your bet.

But first, consider the odds.

CHAPTER ONE

ANTE UP

(A Lesson in Gambling.)

"Place your bets," the table-boss droned in a disinterested monotone he'd murmured a million times as he gave the wheel of fortune a spin.

Five people sat in front of the man. The first was a well-dressed, affluent, take-charge kinda businessman. The second was a nicely groomed, energetic, liberated, New-Age gal (oh, how she hated that word "gal"). The third was a typical good ol' boy with hardly an enemy in the world. The fourth was a religious man dressed in the traditions of his faith. And the fifth, an attractive lady dressed in a gown of humility, a scarf of repentance and a hat of faith. All were watching the disk as it spun, mesmerized by the motion, the flashing lights and the "clackety-clack" sound of the flipper bouncing against the brass posts.

The table-boss wore an old-fashioned green plastic visor on his head, shading his eyes from the lights above; a red garter just above the elbow held up the right sleeve of his starched white shirt. He held a stick that looked like a miniature shepherd's crook and used it to rake markers off the table into a drawer beneath. A Mickey Mouse pattern decorated the red suspenders crisscrossing his back, and a match stick in the corner of his mouth twitched as he silently chewed on its end. "You must place your bets," he added with firmness. "Everybody has to wager. There will be no exceptions to the rule."

Startled back to reality, the five mesmerized observers simultaneously shook the cobwebs from their heads. His words had released them from the hypnosis of the wheel that had held them captive. The wealthy businessman was the first to speak, and he was angry. "I don't have to bet. You can't make me bet. This is a free country. Don't you know who I am? Why, I could buy and sell you a million times over. How dare you tell me that I have to bet. I refuse to play your silly game!"

The table-boss shook his head. He had seen this kind before. "The self-reliant businessman bets 'No Bet,' " he said sadly. The eyes beneath the visor pleaded, silently begging the businessman to change his mind.

He got no response. The match stick twitched nervously in his lips as he pushed the businessman's marker to the shaded "No Bet" area at the center of the table.

Resentment shot back from the executive's eyes as they fired laser beams of hatred toward the croupier. "Nobody tells me what to do," he said with an air of finality. "Nobody!"

The liberated lady hated the entrepreneur for all he stood for—sexism, bigotry, bias and power."Put my marker on 'Reincarnation.' That's where I'll take my chances," she chimed confidently. "I'm bettin' we go around as many times as it takes to get it right." She failed to see her own hypocrisy, but her self-assured look changed to bewilderment when she saw the croupier's face. No longer bored, he looked genuinely worried. That bothered her some, but looks from men failed to move her much.

"And you, sir?" the table-boss asked as he glanced toward the religious man.

"Religion," came the response. "An unfeigned faith will be a winner for sure. I have no doubts. Since I am positive there is a God, I'm sure a sincere seeker will never be condemned by him.

Yes, I think I'll bet it all on 'Religion.' "

Compassion radiated from the face of the table-boss as he placed the man's marker in the area labeled "Religion." The table-master seemed to know something the others didn't. That made the religious man a little nervous, too.

It was now the fourth person's bet. "I've led a good life, been a good husband and tried to be a good father to my kids. I've always attempted to help people. I've been involved in my community, coached Little League teams and I have never cheated or taken anything that wasn't mine. I'm a good man and I'm not aware of ever having made an enemy. Surely a good person will be okay. Place my bet on 'Being a Good Person.' " The table boss obliged, but the expression on his face never changed.

All eyes turned toward the unusually dressed lady. Her wager would be the last.

"I'm a Christian and good Christians don't gamble," she began. "At least I don't think they should—should they?" The eyes of the croupier made her question herself. "It's not right to bet, is it?"

"It's all a gamble, madam. Life's a gamble." The croupier's match stick switched from one side of his mouth to the other as he talked.

"How so?" she asked.

"Life is filled with choices. Choices are nothing more than calculated risks. Taking risks is betting. That makes your decision a gamble. And the only difference between 'faith' and a 'bet' is the odds. The surer you are that you'll win, the more faith you have. When there is no chance of losing, you have the ultimate in faith. As the odds worsen, the wager becomes more of a bet. It's faith when you're sure. It's a bet when you're not." The table-boss rested his case.

That was a new concept to her. After a pause of reflection she spoke softly. "What you're saying sounds true." The lady paused again and thought for a moment, pondering her next words. "However, I'm still not comfortable with wagering. Let me ask you this. What are the stakes? You told us we have to bet but you haven't told us what we have to wager."

"Like I said, lady, you have to bet it all."

"What do you mean?"

His answer was short, and scary. "Your eternal soul!"

He had startled them all.

Four sets of eyes focused intently on the croupier. The fifth pair of eyes were closed in prayer. The four then looked to the praying woman who had not yet placed her bet, and wondered what she would do.

"I will bet on the Christ of the Bible," were her words. "The Book has the least chance of being wrong. So many have unsuccessfully tried to find fault in it for so many years, but it has stood the tests of time and scrutiny. The Bible has a reliability that goes beyond chance. I believe the best odds are to go with God's Word. If I have to bet, and I apparently do, place my marker on Jesus."

The businessman whispered, "Give me a big break." The New-Age lady murmured "Jesus Freak" under her breath. The good ol' boy just stared while the religious man wondered whether liberal theology was right after all. A smile and an affirming nod from the croupier shook him up. The confidence of the other three dropped, too. A couple of them realized their wagers might even be long shots—at best.

"Ladies and gentlemen, as long as the wheel spins you may change your minds and move your markers. However, when it comes to a stop all bets are final. Is that understood?"

All heads nodded, including the businessman's. He had come to the realization that not betting was, in fact, a bet. He was betting that he didn't have to bet—and knew it.

Although their assurance had been shaken, nobody changed a bet. The croupier wasn't surprised. Not many did.[1]

All eyes riveted on the wheel. All but the table-boss. He already knew the outcome. It was always the same.

When the wheel of fortune came to a stop, glances of surprise and looks of concern came over each face as their eyes flashed from one to the other. One person had won. Four had lost. The table-boss didn't even turn around for a look. He knew the wheel always stopped in the same place.

It was then that the croupier reached under the table and opened a drawer. Smoke and sulfur belched upwards, catching everyone off guard. Stench instantly filled the room. The table-master's gartered arm flashed the stick across the table, catching four of the markers in its crook, and proceeded to rake them into the drawer. Four of the gamblers disappeared from the table. They had lost without realizing the magnitude of their bet or the terribly long odds they had chosen.

And the winner? The prize went beyond her wildest dreams.

* * * * * * * *

Look closely. Do you see the table? The one over there with your name at the open seat. You have to sit down. No choice. There is no proceeding on until your bet is on the table.

Feel the softness of the plush cushion beneath you as you settle in. The upright wheel is just behind the table. Notice the guy in the Mickey Mouse suspenders with the red garter on his sleeve.

"Place your bets," the table-boss drones in a disinterested monotone he's murmured a million and one times. He gives the wheel of fortune a spin.

Like it or not, you have to sit down and make a bet. Your can't pass on by. House rules! What are you going to do? Remember the businessman? No bet is really a bet, so not betting isn't an option. On what are you going to wager? What choice will you make?

If the table-boss could advise you, he'd say something like this: When making a bet, always measure upside potential against downside risk. Then consider the odds. When the stakes are high, don't take needless risks. With a lot on the line, never play a hunch. Don't follow your intuition. Forget what your guts say. Go with the odds. Long-shot gamblers are losers.

The Odds

My daddy used to be a bookie. And not only did he take bets on horse races, he also ran card games in the back of the China Lake Tavern before it burned down. Then he switched to the Porthole Bar and Cafe.

I watched many a poker game while I was growing up. I also cleaned cards after school and mopped and waxed the "joint" for spending money. I know something about bars, drunks, cards, dice—and odds.

One night two strangers were in a "low-ball" poker game. That's a game where straights and flushes don't count and the lowest hand wins. When the game had been going on for eighteen hours, my dad took a nap, leaving the game to the dealer. When he awoke, two strangers had most of the money on the table in the form of stacks of chips in front of them. They appeared to be adversaries, but they were really in "cahoots" with each other in a dangerous game of cheating the house and the other players.

Dad saw what was happening right away. The strangers would get in a pot together, sucking in several other players. One would signal the other the card he needed to make his hand. If his partner had it he would signal back. Then when someone finally "called," the player needing a card would put his cards in a stack face down on the table. Before he had time to turn and fan his hand, his partner, who was acting angry, would holler, "Let me see those cards!" Then he would reach out, and with the missing card hidden in his palm, "cap" the other player's stack (put the needed card on top of the unfanned hand). Finally, he would turn the cards and spread them, revealing a very good hand . . . a hand that he had helped to make. The men were cleaning up; the chips piling up in front of them proved it.

My father whispered in the dealer's ear.

The next time the situation happened, three hands hit the table in rapid succession . . . Bang, Bang, Bang! The cheater, after being called, put his cards face down on the table in a stack as usual. His partner's hand reached out with the hidden card in his palm to cap his partner's cards, but before it got there the dealer put his hand on the unfanned stack, covering it. Before the co-conspirator could pull his hand back, he had placed the hidden card on the back of the dealer's hand. The crime had been revealed, and in the world of high-stakes poker men have been killed over much less. There would be hell to pay.

All the players around the table instantly realized what the two men had been doing and stood staring. Eyes spoke volumes. Stares were followed by threats and obscenities. Then a couple of knives appeared. The regulars, who had been had by two "sharpies" from the big city, were ready to take the card sharks out into the desert and kill them. But my dad prevailed and nixed that idea. Instead, he distributed the cheaters' money equally around the table while the locals took the crooks outside, rearranged their teeth and facial features, and sent them back to LA with their tails between their legs in a windowless car that had been severely dented all over.

Those two guys thought the odds were good enough to bet their well-being on the outcome of their scam. They had clearly gotten away with it before (they weren't amateurs) so they thought they could do it again. But they lost. It's not wise to make a big bet on anything but a sure thing.

My daddy made a lot of money off long-shot gamblers over the years. He won; they lost. These days, we hear a great deal about occasional lottery winners, but there wouldn't be enough room in the papers if we started reporting on all the losers. With rare exceptions, long-shot gamblers lose.

> Don't take chances with your well-being.

The Lottery

A few years ago a multi-state Powerball lottery was worth $140 million dollars. The operators sold 200 million tickets.

A guy from Florida won it all on a 200-million-to-1 shot. Not bad for a buck. The real lesson, though, is that there were 199,999,999 losers.

And some wagered away more than they could afford to lose. Before the drawing there were people trading in their retirement money for thousands of dollars worth of tickets in a pathetic effort to favorably alter the odds. Some people sold their homes and put their equity in tickets. It was crazy.

Do you realize how difficult it is to significantly alter the odds with those kinds of numbers and that kind of rake off? Consider this: if you spent 100 million dollars on tickets, you would still have a fifty percent chance of *losing*. But it doesn't matter much if you're only betting a buck.

What if you could bet your life on the lottery, and if you won you received 140 million dollars? But if you lost they killed ya'? Don't you know that we would still have some players . . . but not nearly as many. Why? There is more than a dollar at risk. The stakes just went way up.

Upside/Downside Rule

There is a rule useful in both gambling and business: Always weigh upside potential against downside risk.

You wouldn't buy a stock the experts said was going to decline in value unless you were convinced it would go up. You wouldn't purchase a home in a declining market unless you thought things were going to turn around. You would need some pretty good information to go against the pros and buck the odds, wouldn't you?

How good is your information regarding eternity? Are you going on a gut feeling or what someone told you? Are you going on something a teacher or professor taught you in school? Is your source more reliable than the Bible? Consider what's at stake.

You wouldn't risk your life to save another person without estimating your chances of survival. There isn't a student in the world whose teacher grades on the curve who doesn't look around the room and try to figure the odds of getting the desired grade. *What are my chances of . . . ?* You fill in the blank. We are always looking at odds and balancing upside potential against downside risk. We do it all the time—except when it comes to eternity. Then, for some reason, most people throw the odds out the window and stick their heads in the sand and call their decision intelligent . . . even when the payoff is heaven or hell.

If you risk a dollar it doesn't matter much. But risking a life, now that's something else.

Russian roulette. One bullet, six chambers. What you would bet depends on where the gun is pointed, doesn't it? If it's pointed at the wall I wouldn't mind betting it won't go off. But it's quite another issue if it's pointed at my head. What's worth risking the more than 16 percent chance of death that Russian roulette offers? Saving a loved one? Sure! An operation for incurable cancer? Why not! Lots of money? No way!

Unless you're desperate.

The Desperation Factor

We always weigh gain against loss while considering risk before making choices . . . along with one other factor. Desperation! People who are desperate take more chances than those who are content. If you're content there is no need to take chances.

Who are the ones who do drugs? The desperate and the bored. The desperate want to escape their circumstances. So do those who are bored, because boredom makes you desperate.

Consider what millionaire football hero O. J. Simpson said, long before he was charged with murder, "I sit in my house and sometimes I get so lonely it's unbelievable. Life has been so good to me. I've got a great wife, good kids, money, my own health—and I'm lonely and bored. . . . I often wondered why so many rich people commit suicide. Money sure isn't a cure-all."[2]

Hear the same desperation in famous cartoonist Ralph Barton's suicide note: "I have had few difficulties, many friends, great successes; I have gone from wife to wife, and from house to house, visited great countries of the world, but I am fed up with inventing devices to fill up twenty- four hours of the day."[3]

I remember an old study from my public health days at UCLA that suggested the drug abuse and alcoholism rates, on a per-capita basis, were a full one-third higher among the rich than among the poor. I guess the poor still have their dreams, which makes the rich all the more desperate to find meaning in life. But when money, power and influence don't satisfy, the result is desperation.

What have you put at risk at some point in your life as the result of desperation? Money, goals, desires, dreams, relationships, health, family? Maybe even life itself. I know people who are so afraid of doctors that they would rather have cancer and not treat it than find out they've got it and have to go through the cure. Some people risk the probabilities of contracting a sexually transmitted disease, risking health and death, and ruining their marriage just to fill a desperate need for intimacy. That kind of thinking doesn't make sense to me, but it's the way some folks are wired.

Risk, gain, odds, desperation, boredom—these are a few of the variables that go into decision making. Throw in the rest of what's shaped your personality, plus the consequences of dysfunctional upbringing that's found in so many homes, and it's no wonder there is so much warped thinking. (Actually "dysfunctional" has become a highly overused word. I prefer the word "torqued.") And warped thinking results in weird conclusions, strange decisions and poor choices.

Warped Thinking

My friend Dick had some warped thinking. He chose to play Russian roulette with eternity, and—interestingly enough—God let him get away with it. Let me explain.

Before playing for the Lakers, while coaching at UCLA, I played AAU basketball for the Kitchen Fresh Chippers, a potato chip manufacturer. Dick coached the team. I wasn't into the Lord much in those days, but occasionally I'd have flashes of spirituality. Dick had been raised in church and had a highly committed and godly wife. As a result, Dick knew all the Christian buzz words.

I'd asked him if he was a believer. His response was, "Not yet, I still have a few things I want to do. After I do them I'll accept Christ."

Several years later, after my decision to serve God, Dick's words still burned in my heart. I tracked him down and gave him a call. After the usual hellos, the conversation went something like this:

"Dick, have you received Christ yet?"

"No, not yet, but I'm close."

"What's keeping you?"

"A couple more things to do."

"Is it true that you believe everything the Bible says about Jesus?"

"Yes, absolutely."

"But you won't give your life to him?"

"Not yet."

It was then I posed a hypothetical question. "Dick, what if a truck was coming straight at you on the freeway and a head-on collision was unavoidable?"

"I'd quick pray and receive Christ."

"What if it happened from the rear and you didn't have time to pray?"

His reply totally caught me off guard. "That's a chance I'm willing to take for a while."

"You understand and believe, yet you are willing to toy with eternity because you're not ready to make a commitment? Dick, I don't understand such thinking."

"That's the way it is," were Dick's words of finality.

I called my friend once each year for four years. The fourth call found him having trusted Christ and wondering how he could have been such a fool to have been willing to play such a dangerous game of Russian roulette with eternity. But he played and had won. God was gracious. Dick had changed his bet before the wheel had stopped spinning and he told me Christ was making a wonderful difference in his life. But his example is unusual. I've heard it estimated that only 15-20 percent of all people who come to Christ do so after reaching the age of twenty.

Dick beat the odds. He finally realized that no bet was a bet and that he didn't have good enough reasons for putting off his decision. Besides, his wasn't a shot in the dark kinda thing. He had seen what the Bible had meant to his wife and had seen her change into a person who reflected the image of Jesus Christ. He had all the proof he needed that life in Christ was real, so he finally changed his choice. But until he made that new wager my friend Dick had been a Dagon Dummy.

Dagon Dummies

Sometimes the facts don't change a thing. In 1 Samuel 5:1-12 the Philistines had captured the ark of God. They took it into the temple of their god Dagon and set the ark beside the idol. The next day Dagon was found face down before the ark of the Lord, in a posture of worship.

Phil, the Philistine leader, had the idol returned to its place, but the next morning Dagon was down again. Only this time its head and hands had been broken off.

Then God brought a heavy hand on the area around the Philistine temple in the form of devastation, affliction of young and old, panic, tumors, and death. (Sometimes the Hebrew word for tumor means hemorrhoid. Can you imagine hemorrhoids so bad that thousands were dying? What I wouldn't give to have a corner on the Preparation H market during times like that!) It got so bad the people wanted God's box outta' there. So they gave it back to Israel.

After those events the Philistine folks knew the God of the Ark of the Jews had authority over Dagon. And they clearly acknowledged the heavy hand of God upon them. This God of the Jews was supreme and the people of the land knew it. Word travels fast. "There is no God like the God of the Bible," is the equivalent of their acknowledgment. You know that too, don't you?

The Philistines got rid of the Ark when God sent tumors and death upon them. They knew the source of their troubles. God had gotten their attention. But did the dummies transfer their worship? No way! They stuck with Dagon and bet on a known loser. Why? With Dagon the people wouldn't have to change. But the God of the Jews demanded holiness. Folks throughout history would rather do their own thing than submit to the will of God, even if it means going to hell.

If you're a Dagon Dummy there isn't anything I can say or do that will change your mind. God dumped ten plagues on Pharaoh and the ol' boy never softened up. He had an impossibly hard heart. If that's you, don't waste your time. Stop reading now. But if you still have a tender heart press on and we will consider the next question.

Do you know enough to make your choice wisely? Remember, you want the best possible odds, because this is not a buck you are betting. Your soul is on the line.

Checking Form

Good gamblers do their homework. I had a friend who died in a plane crash a few years ago who had come to Christ years before while running from the Mafia. He had worked up a formula for picking the point spreads in football games. He had several people gathering information and doing research. When the right variables came together Dave consistently beat the Las Vegas odds makers. He was so good casinos stopped taking his bets and he had to hire people to get his bets "down."

The mob wanted his formula. They wined him and dined him and wanted him to become one of their "wise guys." When Dave declined, a "hit" was put out on him. He and his girlfriend ran with a sack full of money and a gun. Dave got saved reading a Gideon's Bible he picked up in a motel in the Dakotas while running from the Mafia. Then he married his girl friend and later become a traveling preacher.

My friend beat the odds in two ways. First, his formula really worked when he did his homework. There aren't many who have a system that really works and changes established odds in their favor.

Dave also beat the odds by outrunning a Mafia hit. He started preaching a few years later and stopped running. A couple of "wise guys" dropped by to hear him and decided to take his name off the list, which is not normally done. Dave had done his homework in the Word and preached it. He'd stopped gambling and wasn't using his formula, so he was no longer considered a threat to the mob. They let him live.

People who regularly play the ponies also do their homework. They are trying to improve their odds. As a kid, I remember meeting the Greyhound bus around midnight each night during the summers. My dad had the racing forms for the next day's horse races sent up to China Lake from Los Angeles each day. People who bet the horses study time, distance, weight, jockey, track conditions—all the factors that go into a horse race. It's called "checking form." They are forecasting the race in an attempt to improve their odds. We called it "prognosticating."

Why would they spend that kind of time and effort? *Because understanding the variables that go into determining the odds is the key to making a good bet.*

Place Your Bet

As I have said, a bet has three basic components (if you can keep desperation out of it)—*how much, on what, at what odds?*

In this game, the bet is your soul and you can't opt out. Everyone has to ante up. Everyone is "in." Like it or not, if the Bible is right, the chip that represents the ownership of your eternal soul is on the line. And no bet is still a bet, because betting you don't have to bet is a bet.

Assuming you have to bet, on what are you going to wager? New Age stuff? Being a good person? Religions? Jesus Christ?

Do your homework before you place your bet. Don't take somebody else's word on this one. Make sure you know if your folks are right or wrong. And your teachers, professors and friends too. There is too much at stake not to. And don't make too many assumptions based on your own thinking either. Our ways are not God's ways and our hearts can't be trusted.[4]

Have you ever made a mistake in your life? Silly question. Of course you have.

Are you aware of God having ever made a mistake? No! I'm not either.

Then how is it that when you disagree with God you conclude that *you* are the one who is right? You are a piece of work, aren't you? Me, too. Talk about being a Dagon Dummy!

Maybe you think being a good person will protect your soul.

How good is good enough? The odds suggest that most nice people will go to hell, because "being nice" has nothing to do with who goes. We certainly weren't born good. Did your parents have to teach you to be bad? No, you picked it up naturally. Need I say more? Who is "good" when compared to the holiness of God? We'll talk about this later on. But even though I don't understand why nice people have to go to hell, and I certainly am repulsed by the concept of eternal torment, my ways are not God's ways—I'm not privy to the information he, and only he, has.

I have his word (the Bible) and I have my thoughts. If I had to bet (and I do), which should I bet on? It's still a stupid question when put that way, isn't it? It is if I think the Bible as God's Word is less reliable than my thinking, but that's the way things are going now.

The odds suggest that betting on yourself, how good you've been, anything you've done or anything you've got are long shots at best as pathways to heaven. Considering what's at stake, I'd call those very bad bets.

Don't Bet on Religion

Religion won't do it either. The Pharisees of Jesus' day were certainly religious. And Christ let it be known that they would be doomed to hell if they didn't change their ways. Serious seekers will not be okay. The odds are sure stacked against them. Jesus' teaching confirms that. "There is no other name by which a man [or woman] can be saved other than the name Jesus Christ."[7]

"But Christianity is a religion." Is that what you're saying? You're right, and when approached as a religion instead of a relationship, it is just as deadly as any other kind of wrong thinking. Jesus made it clear:

> Not everyone who says to Me, 'Lord, Lord,' will enter the kingdom of heaven; but he who does the will of My Father who is in heaven. Many will say to Me on that day, 'Lord, Lord, did we not prophesy in Your name, and in Your name cast out demons, and in Your name perform many miracles?' And then I will declare to them, 'I never knew you; depart from Me, you who practice lawlessness.' (Matthew 7:21–23)

The word "many" means a great number. People who say "Lord, Lord" are those who call themselves Christians. In other words, Jesus said, "A great number of those who call themselves Christians are not born again."

Many will bet on Christianity and lose. Why? Because Christianity as just a religion won't solve anyone's sin problem. Believers want to follow Christ. You can practice a religion, or be associated with one, and not be a follower. Allow me to illustrate.

Assume you are a bride. The pastor asks, "Will you take this woman to have and to hold, in sickness and in health, for richer or poorer, for better or for worse until death you do part? Will you?"

And your groom says, "What do you mean by that? How sick? How poor? How bad?"

Would you continue on with the wedding? Not likely. There is no commitment, and without commitment there is no basis for a deep, long-lasting relationship.

Jesus is saying, "Follow me."

Is your response, "Where?" "How far?" "Under what circumstances?" "Later!"

One of Christ's disciples wanted to take care of a few details at home before he became a follower. "No way," is the essence of Christ's response.[5] Here's the bottom line. There is no basis for a relationship if you are not willing to follow Jesus Christ—right now!

At this point in your pilgrimage you have no idea where that commitment to Christ will take you or a full understanding of what it means. But within the framework of your limited understanding would you be willing to go wherever, whenever and do whatever if you were sure the whole deal is real? Unless you're a Dagon Dummy, your answer will be a resounding, "YES! I'd bet on Jesus."

The odds suggest that only those who have a personal relationship with Christ will win the bet. The basic theme of the Bible would have to be wrong for it not to be so. If the details of the Bible are accurate, can't we conclude that its basic theme must be correct? Of course! Remember, Jesus himself said he was the only way to God.[6] Therefore, considering the stakes, betting against God's Son becomes the longest shot of all and the worst choice you could make.

Setting the Odds

You can bet on almost anything in Las Vegas. The pros study the variables and set the odds. Games, bouts, races, elections, court rulings—there is no end to the bets the Vegas odds makers will take.

Why do you think there is such opulence in their casinos? Because that's where the money stays! Where does that money come from? Gamblers! Who are the winners? The odds makers. Who are the losers? The gamblers.

What does that tell you? *People who wager against the odds ultimately lose.*

The house sets the odds. A few players get lucky and win. The house likes that. It keeps the masses coming back. If everyone lost all the time it wouldn't be a gamble and no one would do it. But in the long run, the house always wins because they set the odds in their favor. In Vegas you have to beat the odds to win. You might do that occasionally by being lucky, but the longer you play, the more impact the odds will have, and ultimately you'll lose.

Therefore, what I'm suggesting is that you do your homework. No serious gambler who plays the ponies would ever make a bet without "checking form."

I've checked form for myself regarding my faith. There is plenty of proof, if you're willing to take a look. We'll look at my favorite reasons in chapter four. I'm convinced you don't have to get a frontal lobotomy to become a follower of Christ.

With so much at stake, playing ostrich and sticking your head in the sands of denial doesn't seem very bright to me. Ignoring reality doesn't change truth. No document has been more highly scrutinized over a longer period of time and stood the test any better than the Bible. Its truth defies the non-believing odds makers.

We shouldn't be surprised. After all, God did author it. It's our operation and maintenance manual. Buy a new car and you'll find a manual in the glove box. Read it and you'll know how to best operate and maintain your new pride and joy. It's the same with the Bible. Read it and you'll know how to best operate and maintain God's pride and joy. After all you are his favorite creation.

Not believing the Bible is a bit like mortgaging your home to buy lottery tickets. The odds stink big time and investing your life savings isn't going to change them. It's the same with hell. You're playing some long odds if you don't believe that place is real and to be avoided at all costs.

Is there anything more valuable than the soul you have to bet?

In this game your soul is the only bet the house will allow, it is what all the players have to bet, and everyone has to play.

And the payoff. What are we playing for? The winners get heaven! And the losers? Hell! The absolute best or the absolute worst. No in-betweens.

My friend, this is the biggest game in town. You won't find a wager where the stakes are any higher. Take my advice and go with the best odds possible. You'll find them in the Bible. Everything else is a long shot at best.

Don't Miss the Point

A guy in a bar was trying to help a drunk break his drinking habit. He took two glasses and filled one with booze. He filled the other with water. Then he took a worm and dropped it in the glass filled with water. The worm swam around and had a good ol' time. After a short while he took the worm out of the water and dropped it in the booze. The creature died in a matter of moments.

"There," said the man, feeling like he'd really illustrated something profound, "What does that prove?"

The drunk responded, "You'll never have worms if you drink a lot of booze."

He had missed the point completely.

Don't miss the point. I'm not suggesting you become a gambler. I'm not advocating playing the lottery, betting on horse races, going to Las Vegas or becoming a card player. But life is a gamble and requires a wager. Your soul. And since no bet is a bet, go with the odds. Choose Christ.

It's Post Time

At the horse track a guy in a red coat, tight riding pants and black boots takes his trumpet and proclaims "It's Post Time!" on his horn. The blood of the regular bettors starts to pump. The

horses come onto the track and walk around a bit before entering
the gate. A few last-minute bets are placed as the wagering win-
dows close. The final odds are set. Then, blaring over the loud-
speakers, comes the sound that sets the hearts of those who are
into horses on fire, "They're off and running!"

You have placed your bet. If you didn't bet, you are betting
that you don't have to bet. Either way your soul is on the line.
The question is, "On what or on whom are you betting and what
are the odds?" If you have a two-hundred-million-to-one chance
of winning you have made a long-shot gamble. At those odds you
are probably going to lose. If you have a two-hundred-million-to-
one chance of losing you have a lot of faith. You are probably
going to win.

> With what you know about the Bible, what are the
> odds of its main themes being wrong? If your beliefs
> are contrary to the Bible, what are the odds of you
> being right and the Bible being wrong?

Remember, you are betting your soul. Hell is the payoff for
losing. With that kind of risk, your best bet is the bet with the
best odds. To determine your odds you need to "check form." You
need to study and understand the variables that go into this
wager. In the next chapter we'll examine enough singular facts
that—when considered together—should form a basis for you to
place your bet. If the harmony of the data goes beyond the realm
of chance, you won't have to go with a long shot. You'll have
faith and you can make your choice with complete confidence. I
think you'll find that you don't have to get a frontal lobotomy to
become a believer.

CHAPTER TWO

YOU DON'T NEED A FRONTAL LOBOTOMY TO BELIEVE

(Formulating a basis for your bet.)

Do the facts support the Bible as being the word of God?

What about this guy called Jesus?

How real is the whole Christian deal?

Those are the issues, aren't they?

Considering the consequences of being wrong (hell), if we can reasonably establish that the deal is real, then only a fool would reject eternal life in favor of an eternity in hell. Only a fool or someone who didn't want to submit to God's authority (same thing).

Let's start with God and see if the facts suggest his existence. Understand that volumes have been written in defense of the Christian faith. In the pages that follow I just want to skim the surface of what makes the most sense to me and share a few of my favorite reasons as to why the odds overwhelmingly support a bet on the whole deal being real.

Is the Bible for Real?

There are as many as forty ancient books claiming to be a superior revelation. All of the others talk about God. In the Bible God talks.

The first book in the Old Testament is Genesis; in the first chapter you'll find "God said" nine times. The statement, "thus says the Lord" appears twenty-three times in the last Old Testament book (Malachi). In between, the phrase "the Lord spoke" appears five hundred and sixty times in the first five books alone. Isaiah claims that his message came from the Lord more than forty times, Ezekiel sixty times and Jeremiah a hundred times. "The Lord spoke" or "the Lord says" appears more times than I cared to count. Pratney says the words "the Lord spoke" or phrases similar occur thirty-eight hundred times.[7] The actual number is 3,808.[8]

MacArthur says, "There are three hundred and twenty direct quotes from the Old Testament in the New Testament. Jesus Christ added his validation as well, by quoting from twenty-four Old Testament books. Consider the impact of Christ's endorsement:

> When examining the testimony of Jesus about the Scriptures, we have to accept one of three possibilities. The first is that there are no errors in the Old Testament, just as Jesus taught. Second, there are errors, but Jesus didn't know about them. Third, there are errors and Jesus knew about them, but He covered them up.
>
> If the second is true—that the Old Testament contains errors of which Jesus was unaware—then it follows that Jesus was a fallible man, he obviously wasn't God and we can dismiss the whole thing. If the third alternative is true—that Jesus knew about the errors but covered them up—then he wasn't honest, he wasn't holy, he certainly wasn't God, and again, the entire structure of Christianity washes away like a sand castle at high tide.
>
> I accept the first proposition—that Jesus viewed the Old Testament as the Word of God, authoritative and without error.[9]

New Testament writers refer to the Old Testament some one thousand times in all. "There can be little doubt that the New Testament writers believed that the Old Testament was God's revelation—his inspired Word."[10] But they also knew that what they were writing was God's revelation as well.

There was a four-hundred-year silence between the last book of the Old Testament and the coming of the first New Testament prophet, John the Baptist. Jesus said that John was greater than any of the Old Testament prophets. Then He went on and said that the New Testament prophets would do even greater works than John. Jesus Christ personally validated the words of those who qualified as New Testament writers.

The N.T. authors knew they were writing God's word, too. They said so. Luke, Peter, Paul and John all validated their words as being from God, and went on to add their stamp of approval on what the others had written. That makes the New Testament just as valid as the Old. It is clear, from the first to the last book, God spoke enough times to validate the Bible as being his word. And Jesus Christ confirmed it as well.

My Favorite Reasons for the Bible Being Real

Authors McDowell and Stewart made an interesting proposal to illustrate how miraculous the authorship of the Bible really is:

> If you selected ten people living at the same time in history, living in the same basic geographical area, with the same basic educational background, speaking the same language, and you asked them to write independently on their conception of God, the result would be anything but a united testimony.
>
> It would not help if you asked them to write about man, woman or human suffering, for it is the nature of human beings to differ on controversial subjects. However, the biblical writers not only agree on these subjects but on dozens more. They have

complete unity and harmony. There is only one story in the Scriptures from beginning to end, although God used different human authors to record it. The supernatural character of the Bible is one reason we believe Christianity to be true.

Consider the evidence of the hand of God that's revealed in the harmony of the variables surrounding the Bible. It's not one book. Did you know that? It's sixty-six books and they were written by forty authors, including two kings, two priests, a physician, two fishermen, two shepherds, a legalistic theologian, a statesman, a tax collector, a soldier, a scribe, a butler, and twenty-five others from equally diversified backgrounds ranging from peasants and poets to statesmen and scholars. They wrote in the wilderness, from dungeons and palaces, in exile, both in wartime and peacetime, over a period of sixteen hundred years, in several countries, on three continents, in three languages, on hundreds of controversial subjects.

However, even with all of these variables, this Book of books is in perfect harmony with itself and remains in precise agreement with all other factual, historical, archaeological, and scientific works, both current and past. The Bible contains flashes of inspired poetry as well as detailed history, captivating biography, letters, memoirs, and prophetic writings—yet it speaks with astonishing continuity, miraculous accuracy and tells one unfolding story . . . God's redemption of man.

The harmony of the variables goes beyond the realm of chance. How is it then that the Bible remains in harmony with itself, in spite of the information explosion and its superhighway? The odds suggest the hand of God at work. All other bets are long shots.

The Holy Bible is a miracle of God's preservation that can't be denied. I might bet a buck that the Bible is not God's word, if I had a dollar I didn't mind throwing away. But I would never bet my soul. The odds on the Bible not being true are too remote.

Imagine pulling sixty-six published works from forty different authors. What would you have. Agreement? Hardly! You'd have hodgepodge!

Add that the documents are to be written in three different languages. Will that make the writings more likely to be in harmony? No way! That makes it a lot tougher.

How about the authors having to write on three different continents and from several different countries without phones or faxes. You say, "Jay, you're making this impossible." You're right. But let's send the probabilities off the chart.

What if you spread the writings out over sixteen hundred years? Does that add to the confusion? Sure! It's just like taking the plane with the letters spelling *Playing the Odds: Eternity's Your Choice* from one thousand feet to fifteen thousand feet and dropping them. Spreading the writing over that much time would make agreement among the writers a miracle. Exactly! Since miracles come from God, that's where the Bible came from.

If the Bible really came from God, since he is all knowing, shouldn't it be accurate scientifically, historically and archaeologically? If God wrote it, shouldn't it pass the triple test?

The Triple Test of Trustworthiness

Of the forty ancient books of "superior revelation" there is only one that stands the triple test of trustworthiness: The Bible.

Test One: The Scientific Test

Can you imagine any work of antiquity not contradicting science? Me neither. There are few books more than five years old that have anything to say about science that don't contradict what was formerly thought credible.

While the Koran said the world was a flat tabletop held up by three elephants and a turtle (and never told us what the turtle stood on), God called it a sphere (Isaiah 40:21–22) and said it hung in nothingness (Job 26:7).

It was the sixteenth century before science discovered the workings of our circulatory system. The Bible had said all along that the life of the flesh is in the blood (Genesis 9:4).

The hydrological cycle was put forth by Isaiah. "As the rain and the snow come down from heaven, and do not return to it without watering the earth and making it bud and flourish, so that it yields seed for the sower and bread for the eater . . ." (55:10)

The principle of land mass being balanced by water mass (isostasy) was spoken of by Isaiah as well (40:12).

It's hard to believe that a book written so long ago doesn't contradict current scientific discovery. Isn't it? John MacArthur noted, "God wrote the Bible for men of all ages and while his Word never contradicts science, it also never gets trapped into describing some precise scientific theory that becomes outdated in a few years, decades or centuries."[11] Josh McDowell observed the same thing but reported it with a twist, "Where the Bible speaks on matters of science, it does so with simple yet correct terms, not absurdities. Where non-biblical accounts of the formation of the universe and other scientific matters border on the ridiculous, the Scriptures nowhere are guilty of this. It is not what could be expected from a book written by men during pre-scientific times."[12] He's right. Men couldn't have done that. Neither could women. The Bible is not the result of natural inspiration. Its inspiration is divine.

Keep in mind that science has made some as-yet unproved claims that are contrary to the Bible. Godless evolution is one of those conclusions. If someone does create life in a test tube (and someone probably will) it won't be evidence for evolution. It will only show how much intelligence is actually required to create life. How many minds have been working on that project for how many years? But creating life in all of its forms was just another day at the office for God. "'Tweren't no big thang."

Not only is the Bible scientifically accurate, it is also histor ically correct. We don't have to be concerned with the accuracy of either Testament. They are right on.

Test Two: The Historical Test

When the Bible was copied, letters were counted, both forward and backward, and measurements were taken from corner to corner to make sure spacing and punctuation were perfect. If a mistake was made, the page was thrown out, not corrected.

The discovery of the Dead Sea Scrolls confirmed how meticulous the Jewish scribes were in the copying of the texts. Only a few minor copyist errors were found between what we have today and the scrolls that were uncovered. No credibility issues resulted from the discoveries. Your Bible, if it's a legitimate translation, is miraculously close to the original. God has kept it intact.

Skeptics don't argue with the historicity of the Bible any more. Dates, places, and occurrences are all right on the money and have been confirmed by archeology. The Old Testament is historically correct. So is the New Testament.

Josh McDowell, in his classic *Evidence That Demands a Verdict*, reports on his findings regarding the New Testament:

> No other document of antiquity even begins to approach such numbers and attestation. In comparison, *The Iliad* by Homer is second with only 643 manuscripts that still survive. The first complete preserved text of Homer dates from the 13th century.
>
> There are now more than 5,300 known Greek manuscripts of the New Testament. Add over 10,000 Latin Vulgate and at least 9,300 other early versions and we have more than 24,000 manuscript copies of portions of the New Testament in existence today.
>
> John Warwick Montgomery says that 'to be skeptical of the resultant text of the New Testament

books is to allow all of classical antiquity to slip into obscurity, for no documents of the ancient period are as well attested bibliographically as the New Testament.'

Sir Frederic Kenyon reports that 'The interval between the dates of original composition and the earliest extant evidence becomes so small as to be in fact negligible, and the last foundation for any doubt that the Scriptures have come down to us substantially as they were written has now been removed. Both the authenticity and the general integrity of the books of the New Testament may be regarded as finally established.'[13]

The accuracy of the New Testament is confirmed by the variety of versions of manuscripts and by the contemporary historical writers of the time. McDowell and Stewart added their stamp of approval with the following endorsement:

The history recorded in the Scriptures also proves to be accurate. As far as we have been able to check them out, the names, places and events mentioned in the Bible have been recorded accurately.[14]

Both the Old and New Testaments have been established to be historically correct, making the Bible accurate in its portrayal of times, dates and places. They both pass the historical test.

History offers more data than archeology can confirm, but archeology is a way to confirm a portion of the Bible's historical accuracy and comprises our third test.

Third Test: The Archaeological Test

For years there was no archaeological record of the Hittites. People called the Bible wrong. Then an archaeologist discovered their capital city, thousands of texts, the Hittite code and we came to the realization that their empire had been vast.

Over the years skeptics maintained that Solomon was broke, that there was no such place as Sodom or Gomorrah and that Belshazzar never existed. Solomon's wealth was confirmed between 1925 and 1934. Tablets have been uncovered confirming the existence of Sodom and Gomorrah. Belshazzar was for real. Archaeological discoveries provided the proof.

There are literally hundreds of volumes on this kind of stuff. Josh McDowell has read most of them and has compiled the opinions of the "biggies" in the field. His conclusion: "So far, the findings of archaeology have verified, and in no case disputed, historical points of the biblical record."[15]

The Bible passes the archaeological test with flying colors. Go to any archaeological dig in the Middle East.

You'll find a searcher with a Bible in one hand and a shovel in the other. When God said, "It's over there," diggers have learned to look over there.

There are more tests than the triple test of trustworthiness. I like the next one most of all. I guess it's because, as you know, I was raised as a "bookie's kid" and I get into odds. Let's look at the test of fulfilled prophecy.

The Test of Fulfilled Prophecy

In the "olden days" if you wanted to draw attention to yourself you would say "thus sayeth the Lord" and everybody would do that old E. F. Hutton routine and stop doin' what they were doin' to listen. People wanted to know what God said in those days. Note that I didn't say they wanted to *do* what he said. But they did want to *know*. I guess that's why everybody wanted to be a prophet. It could be a real power position.

There was a little problem with being a prophet, though. If you were wrong they killed you. That's why there weren't many prophets collecting social security. Only the ones God chose lived that long. But not all of God's prophets got old. If the people didn't like what God said, sometimes they would kill the prophet.

Whether or not they liked what he had to say, the folks found that God was never wrong. For example, God said the coastal city of Tyre would fall and never be rebuilt, and that its timbers and rubble would be thrown into the sea. "Fishermen will dry their nets where the city used to be," that's what God said. But Tyre was a fortified city. "Impossible!" the people shouted. "Tyre will never fall."

Then along came Alexander the Great. He laid siege to Tyre, but the people escaped to a nearby island. Alexander brought in hundreds of slaves, tore down the town, chucked the debris into the water forming a causeway, marched out to the island and snuffed the folks. The foundation of the city of Tyre was scraped clean. Even though there are fresh water springs there (it's a perfect place for a city), you'll still only find fisher-men's nets drying in the sun. Why? 'Cause God said so.

Prophets of God said Babylon would destroy Jerusalem. Come on now! Girl Scouts aren't going to defeat Desert Storm troops. That's the way things were when the prophecy was made. But it happened. God said it would.

My favorite examples of the accuracy of God's word are the Old Testament prophecies that were fulfilled with the coming of Christ. There are more than three hundred, but many are fairly general in nature. Sixty-one are quite specific:

Christ would be betrayed by a friend. Not a political leader or an acquaintance.

The betrayal would be for silver, not gold.

For thirty pieces, not forty.

He would ride, not walk.

Into Jerusalem, not some other city.

On a donkey, not a horse.

The donkey would be female, not male.

And on and on for sixty-one such prophecies.[16] Keep in

mind that Christ had no control over his place, time or manner of birth, his betrayal, manner of death, the people's reactions, the piercing of his side, or his burial. Yet, each phophecy was specifically proclaimed. And at a point in time, in a town that was close to what was then considered the center of the world, one man defied the odds and made the prophecies of several authors writing at least twelve hundred years apart, and (at the least) four hundred years before it was to happen, come true.

A mathematician computed the odds of eight of the prophecies occurring by chance. The probability is 1 in 10 to the 17th power. That's silver dollars two feet deep covering Texas, with one marked, and a blindfolded man walking in at random, bending over, and snagging the marked one on the first try.[17]

The same math man ran the numbers on forty-eight prophecies occurring by chance. The number is 1 in 10 to the 157th power. That's a cubic inch of electrons with one marked and getting it right on the first try. By the way, at 250 per minute, it would take nineteen million years to count one inch of electrons. Counting a cubic inch would require nineteen million times nineteen million times nineteen million or 6.9 times 10 to the 21st power years.[18]

I guess he quit after forty-eight. I can't imagine what sixty-one would do. But then I had trouble visualizing just eight!

Being a gambler's kid, that did it for me. I'm not going to bet against those kind of odds. Are you?

If the Book that tells me about the coming together of sixty-one prophecies also tells me nice people really do go to hell, what am I gonna' do? Am I going to pick and choose what I'm going to believe and what I'm going to discount? No! I've been wrong too many times to do that.

If the Book has always been right, then what is the likelihood that any significant part of it is wrong? Highly unlikely? No—that's not strong enough language. How about *impossible?*

Go with the Odds—Trust the Book

If a horse ran in ninety-nine races and won each time, would you bet against him in the hundredth?

You probably said, "No, sir!"

But if you're a gambler you would reply, "It depends on the odds."

That's the way we are. We will bet against the odds if we think the return is good enough. That's how duped we really are. We think that having our own way is worth going against those kind of odds. Frank Sinatra made "I Did It My Way" a popular song some years ago. It is the boastful life-statement of a fool. He thinks what he's done and his legacy when he's gone will have been worth defying God. He bet against the odds and thinks he's won. And then comes death and eternity. Poor Frank.

Don't go your way. You'll lose for sure. Trust God. Only then will you trust your Bible. Consider the following:

> If God is our ultimate authority and his charac-
> ter is flawless, and if he inspired the writers of
> Scripture to put down his thoughts while still allow-
> ing them freedom of personal expression, then the
> Bible (in its original form) is flawless and it becomes
> our ultimate authority—our only rule for faith and
> practice.[19] [words in parenthesis mine]

The Bible is a book you can count on. McDowell and Stewart conclude:

> The text of the Bible has been transmitted
> accurately. We may rest assured that what we have
> today is a correct representation of what was original-
> ly given. For example, there is more evidence for the
> reliability of the text of the New Testament as an
> accurate reflection of what was initially written than
> there is for any thirty pieces of classical literature put
> together.[20]

You might not understand the Bible right away, but it's trustworthy. For a little leap of faith, you win eternity in Paradise. Billy Graham's whole ministry changed when he made his leap of faith:

> I believe it is not possible to understand everything in the Bible intellectually. One day some years ago I decided to accept the Scriptures by faith. There were problems I could not reason through. When I accepted the Bible as the authoritative Word of God—by faith—I found immediately that it became a flame in my hand. That flame began to melt away unbelief in the hearts of many people and to move them to decide for Christ. The Word became a hammer, breaking up stony hearts and shaping men into the likeness of God. Did not God say, 'I will make my words in thy mouth fire' (Jeremiah. 5:14), and 'Is not my word like as a fire?' saith the Lord; 'and like a hammer that breaketh the rock in pieces?' (Jeremiah. 23:29).

> I found that I could take a simple outline, then put a number of Scripture quotations under each point, and God would use it mightily to cause men to make full commitment to Christ. I found that I did not have to rely upon cleverness, oratory, psychological manipulation, apt illustrations, or striking quotations from famous men. I began to rely more and more upon Scripture itself and God blessed it. I am convinced through my travels and experience that people all over the world are hungry to hear the Word of God.[21]

Add the proof of changed lives; the phenomenon of having a conscience; the calendar being split in two (B.C. and A.D.) by one person; Jesus Christ being the only name that's a cuss word (you never hear anyone swear "Mother Teresa!" or "Mahatma

Ghandi!" or "Martin Luther King!"); the Cross being the world-wide symbol for compassion, and the Bible being the best-selling, the most widely studied and clearly the most closely criticized and scrutinized book in the history of the world; and you ought to have a clue that this deal is real. If it were all a myth, it wouldn't have made such an impact.

What to Do with a Real Deal

As a people, Americans know the Bible is unique. As a nation we cherish it. But esteeming is different than *following*. To follow we have to know what the Bible says. Although most homes have at least one Bible someplace, few people have read it enough to know what it says. Gallup confirms that statement, "Americans revere the Bible—but, by and large, they don't read it. And because they don't read it, they have become a nation of biblical illiterates."[22] Although four in five Americans believe the Bible to be inspired by God, only 15 percent read it daily.[23] Gallup uses strong language when it comes to college graduates, "Particularly shocking is the lack of knowledge of the Bible among college graduates."[24] And he indicates that things are only going to get worse. Three in ten teenagers do not know why Easter is celebrated. Twenty percent who regularly attend religious services don't know any more about Easter than do those who don't.[25]

It's hard to know what God wants you to do if you don't read his instruction manual.

I remember a Calvin and Hobbes cartoon. They were running around throwing a ball, sliding and hitting. It was baseball for two. Calvin asked Hobbes, "Are you out, or am I?"

Hobbes reply was classic, "It depends which game we are playing."

Since so few have read the rule book, most people have decided to make up their own rules and play their own game. In their rather crass book *The Day America Told the Truth*, Patterson and Kim discuss the new moral authority in America. They conclude—the authority is *you*:

> It's the wild, wild West all over again in America, but it's wilder and woollier this time. You are the law in this country. Who says so? You do, pardner.
>
> In the 1950s and even in the early 1960s, there was something much closer to a moral consensus in America. It was mirrored in a parade of moralizing family TV programs: Ozzie and Harriet, Father Knows Best, Donna Reed, Leave It to Beaver, and even Bonanza.
>
> There is absolutely no moral consensus at all in the 1990s. Everyone is making up their own personal moral codes—their own Ten Commandments.
>
> Here are ten extraordinary commandments for the 1990s. These are real commandments, the rules that many people actually live by. (The percentage of people who live by each commandment is included.)

1. I don't see the point in observing the Sabbath (77%).

2 I will steal from those who won't really miss it (74%).

3. I will lie when it suits me, so long as it doesn't cause any real damage (64%).

4. I will drink and drive if I feel that I can handle it. I know my limit (56%).

5. I will cheat on my spouse—after all, given the chance, he or she will do the same (53%).

6. I will procrastinate at work and do absolutely nothing about one full day in every five. It's standard operating procedure (50%).

7. I will use recreational drugs (41 percent).

8. I will cheat on my taxes—to a point (30%).

9. I will put my lover at risk of disease. I sleep around a bit, but who doesn't (31%).

10. [Author's note—number 10 was too tacky. I left it out.]

Almost all of us have highly individualized moral menus like that today. We decide what's right and wrong. Most Americans have no respect for what the law says.[26]

Most people don't treat the Bible as if it is God's personal word to them. But it is. The odds confirm that conclusion. That makes what it says about Christ to be truth.

In this chapter I shared a few of the apologetics that have been meaningful to me. (Don't get confused by the word "apologetic." I'm not apologizing for anything. It's a word that means "defending the faith in a formal presentation.") So much has been written over the years. My desire was to convey a few of my favorites so you could "check form" and have enough information to set the odds and make a good choice. But now it's time to press on with the consequences of making a bad bet—before your marker is pushed into the drawer where the sulfur and smoke belch and burn.

But before studying death and the eternity that follows, there are two principles I want to examine. Mister Spock had an interesting way of teaching one of them. We'll learn the other from Captain Kirk. If you're not a "Trekkie" don't freak out. Kick back, relax and allow yourself to enjoy a couple chapters of "kinda far-out fun" There are valuable lessons to be learned from "Star Trek."

CHAPTER THREE

A LESSON FROM MISTER SPOCK

(You can trust a Vulcan—nice people really do go to hell.)

If I were to use the names Kirk, Spock, Scotty, Dr. McCoy, Uhura, Chekov, and Sulu, would you know what I was talking about?

You can learn a lot from once-Captain (now Admiral) James T. Kirk and his first officer, Mister Spock. To his surprise, Kirk made the discovery that nice people really do go to hell, because that's where Mister Spock went, and he was a nice person. That realization changed the admiral's life and cost him a great deal—in both instances, more than he ever dreamed possible. We have to go back to the movie "Star Trek II" to begin the story.

"Star Trek II: The Wrath of Kahn"

A severely wounded Kahn is in the disabled Starship Reliant. Kirk has won again. But Kahn has activated the Genesis device and in four minutes the biggest explosion man has ever made will occur. A planet will be created in the aftermath of the blast, along with a shock wave that will travel millions of miles before losing its energy.

Of course Kahn will die, but he thinks suicide is worth it because Kirk will be killed in the process. Oh, how Kahn hates

Kirk, his nemesis and enemy. Death for himself will not be too great a price to pay, as long as he can take Kirk with him.

The good captain is aboard the Starship Enterprise, attempting to flee from the blast that will destroy him, his crew, and his beloved ship. But running is an exercise in futility because the warp drive, which allows them to exceed the speed of light, was damaged during the battle with Kahn, and isn't opera-tive. Kirk's spaceship is proceeding along under sluggish impulse power, but it is going too slowly to escape the shock wave that will be coming. Without warp drive the result of the forthcoming detonation will engulf and destroy them.

The engine room is filled with radiation. Repairs to the warp drive are therefore impossible. Anyone who enters will die before a fix can be performed. That is, anyone who has red blood. But Spock is a Vulcan. His blood is green. He'll have more time.

There is no time to argue, so First Officer Spock leaves the bridge without notifying his best friend Admiral Kirk. (We are used to his being a captain from the TV series. He didn't make admiral until "Star Trek II." He'll always be Captain Kirk to me, so that's what I'll call him from now on.) Spock enters the engine room knowing it will bring certain death. He works in agony, but before falling to the floor, the first officer repairs the system and restores warp power just in time. (What a guy!)

From the bridge, Kirk engages the rehabilitated rocketry; he shifts into warp drive just as the Genesis device explodes, and the Enterprise blasts off to safety, outrunning the shock wave. All is well. Hooray!

But what of Spock?

Realizing what has happened, Kirk dashes to the engine room, deeply concerned for the welfare of his best friend. As the captain enters, his first officer is on the other side of a Plexiglas safety shield, dying of radiation poisoning. (Of course, everyone knows Plexiglas is effective in controlling radiation, so we don't have a problem with that. Sure!)

"Is the ship safe?" Spock asks, his face showing the developing sores of the radiation at work.

A simple "Yes" is the captain's reply.

The collapsed Spock crawls over to the Plexiglas wall opposite the captain. The expiring exec's eyes meet Kirk's as he speaks, "Don't grieve, Admiral, it is logical. The needs of the many outweigh . . . "

Kirk cuts him off in mid-sentence as he finishes Spock's words, ". . . the needs of the few."

Spock then quickly adds to Kirk's statement, " . . . or the one."

Continuing, the dying officer concludes, "I have been and always will be your friend."

The first officer holds up his hand to do one of those finger-moving "live-long-and-prosper" routines and presses his palm against the glass in the failing gesture of a farewell handshake. In response, Kirk presses his hand against Spock's with only the Plexiglas separating them. (It's an almost touching moment.)

Only Mr. Spock's green blood has sustained him this long. Any red-blooded man would have died minutes ago. However, the scene can't go on forever, so after a few more groans and gasps Spock rolls over and dies.

Kirk tries to wrap it all up with a final statement of mourning, "Of all the souls I have encountered in my travels, his was the most human." (That was supposed to be a compliment, but it sounded racist to me.)

But Dr. McCoy attempts to one-up the admiral with a final-final comment, "He's really not dead as long as we remember him."

It is then that the movie is drawn to a close, but the finish is pretty lame. Everyone is appropriately sad, of course. Scotty plays "Amazing Grace" on his bagpipes (give me a break) while a black photon torpedo shell is used as a coffin for Spock's body and is rocketed down to the Genesis planet. The new planet is considered a fitting final resting place for the first officer, but the whole thing is more than a little "hokey."

Quite frankly, Trekkies around the world were devastated at the loss of Spock. Just as Batman fans lost their Robin, Star Trek fans suffered at the demise of their pointy-eared hero. But such are the ways of show biz'.

However, don't let your disappointment cause you to forget the central theme of the movie.

> When it comes to life and death, the needs of the many outweigh the needs of the few or the one.

We have only one interest in "Star Trek II"—logic. Disregard their statements about Genesis being ancient myth. (The cast obviously didn't read their Bibles.) All you need to know is that Vulcans are extremely logical. So much so they are devoid of emotion. Also, they can't lie. Never in recorded Trek history has a Vulcan ever told a lie. When a Vulcan says something you can make book on it. You can trust whatever is said.

"When it comes to life and death, the needs of the many outweigh the needs of the few or the one." Now that's logical. If everyone is going to die, and if through the earlier death of one person the rest can be saved, then why not let one die? Since Spock's green blood had the necessary chemistry to keep him alive long enough to make the repairs, and since he had the knowledge needed to complete the task, he was the logical choice. But notice, no one else said, "Spock, go kill yourself so that we might live." It was a decision he made on his own. He understood. In that set of circumstances (life and death), the lives of the majority outweighed the life of the one. It's logical.

When it comes to life and death, the needs of the many

outweigh the needs of the few or the one. In military situations generals use this principle in decision making all the time. If the giving or taking of a comparatively few lives now will save a lot more lives later, it's a good thing to do. That's Spock's principle. Keep it in mind as we leave "Star Trek II" and move on to "Star Trek III."

"Star Trek III: In Search of Spock"

Kirk, who is with his friend Dr. McCoy, is uneasy and wonders why. He hears a voice, "Jim, help me. You left me on Genesis. Why did you do that? Help me. Help me Jim, take me home." Dr. McCoy was the one who had been speaking, but it had been Spock's voice. Weird! Strange!

All this is too much for the good doctor. He collapses and is hospitalized. But James T. Kirk is beginning to get the message. There's unfinished business on Genesis. He has to get Spock back to Vulcan, although he doesn't know why.

That's a problem, though. The Federation has made Genesis a quarantined planet and a forbidden subject. But Kirk tries anyhow. He goes to Federation Headquarters. "Can I borrow the Enterprise to get Spock out of hell?" he asks.

"For a religious trip? Don't be silly," was their response. "You know our policy on issues regarding the separation of church and state."

We find a rejected James Kirk at his condo in San Francisco, near Federation Headquarters. It takes a lot more makeup to make him look young. (What's the similarity between Kirk's face and a ski slope? Ten inches of base and two inches of powder.) He is no longer a starship captain and he doesn't like it much. Flying a desk is not at all like commanding a starship. And being an admiral isn't enough compensation.

The doorbell rings. Upon answering, Kirk finds himself face to face with the Vulcan Ambassador Sarek, who just happens to be Spock's father. Sarek, a full-blooded Vulcan, begins the conversation abruptly, "Why did you bury my son on the Genesis planet?" (I'll be paraphrasing from here on. It's more fun.)

"He died near there and it seemed like a good place to bury him," was Captain Kirk's surprised reply.

"Didn't he tell you?"

"Tell me what?"

Sarek shocked Kirk with his reply, "Didn't my son tell you of the necessity of returning his body to Vulcan? If his body isn't returned he'll spend eternity in a timeless void—the Vulcan equivalent of your hell."

"Really?" exclaimed a stunned Kirk.

"Really," confirmed the somber Vulcan.

"Are you kiddin' me?" Kirk was double checking.

"You know better than that. Vulcans don't kid."

"Oh, that's right. And you can't lie either. It's against your nature isn't it?"

The slow, methodical up-and-down nod of the elder Vulcan's head confirmed what Kirk knew to be true. So did the burning sincerity of his eyes.

Did Captain Kirk believe Spock's father was telling the truth, or did he think this man was controlled by religious superstition? Did he really believe that his good friend would spend eternity in the Vulcan equivalent of hell, or could he be content with the Genesis planet being the final resting place for his best friend? I think we can tell by what Kirk did.

Our actions confirm our beliefs and demonstrate our values. What we say gives some clues to our beliefs, but what we do usually confirms them. So it was with Kirk.

After going to Federation headquarters and getting rejected, Kirk recruited all of his friends. He convinced them of the future facing Spock.

> A person will try to persuade his friends if an issue is
> important enough. That's why someone probably
> gave you this book.

Scotty, McCoy, Sulu, Uhura, and Chekov must have
believed Captain Kirk too, because they all risked career, court
martial, jail and dishonorable discharge. They willingly put everything they had stood for all their lives in jeopardy. Mister Spock's
friends put it all on the line for him. And why not? They were
convinced he was in hell.

Since they couldn't get permission to use the Enterprise,
they "hot-wired" the great Starship Enterprise and swiped it.
Scotty had even gone so far as to sabotage the Excelsior, the only
ship in the galaxy capable of catching them. But that wasn't all.
The crew Kirk recruited passed the second greatest test for belief I
know of—risking their lives—by fighting Klingons. It was Kirk
who had to pass the greatest test of all—listening as his son was
killed by a Klingon.

Can you think of anything Kirk and his friends didn't put at
risk? I can't either. They must have believed rather strongly, don't
you think? More than that, they were resolute. Did they demonstrate commitment and allegiance? You bet! They didn't just sit
like frogs on a log believing they could swim. They jumped in and
proved it. Those people believed that Spock, as nice as he was, was
in hell. You can tell how much people believe by what they do.

By the way, the end of this movie was lousy, too. There is a
questionable ceremony that smacks of satanism, along with some
inappropriate biblical references. But when they finally deliver
Spock's body back to Vulcan, someone asks Kirk, "Why did you
do it?"

It goes without saying that you don't want to get your theology from the movies. Nevertheless, Captain Kirk's answer was a
theological bombshell.

> "When it comes to eternity, the needs of the one out-
> weigh the needs of the many."

Hmmmmmmmm!

Together the two movies made a dramatic statement. Spock showed us that with life and death on the line, the needs of the many outweigh the needs of the few or the one. But with eternity on the line, Captain Kirk showed us that the needs of the one facing hell outweigh the needs of all those going to heaven. And all of a sudden I understood the biblical parable of the ninety-nine sheep and one (Luke 15:4-7). But we're getting ahead of ourselves. We'll deal with that in the next chapter.

Captain Kirk had incorrectly assumed that someone as good as Mister Spock would go to heaven. That's why his encounter with Spock's dad was so surprising. But the captain came away understanding and believing Vulcans go to hell if their bodies aren't returned to the planet Vulcan—and it doesn't matter how nice they were while they lived. As illogical as it seemed, it was true. Vulcans can't lie. And neither does the Word of God. You can trust a Vulcan, and you can trust the Bible.

> Whether a person goes to heaven or hell
> depends on something other than
> how they lived their lives.

It's important to spend eternity in the right place. Hell is to be avoided. Heaven is the place to be. And having been a good person didn't save Spock. Kirk understood.

No matter how terrific an individual is while living, when he dies, he risks going to hell because being nice is not one of the requirements for staying out. Spock didn't meet the prerequisites and Kirk and his crew understood. Their nice friend was really in hell. So risking their lives—and in Kirk's case, even losing his son—seemed worth doing to get Spock out of hell.

Of course, there's a difference between Star Trek and real life—when humans get sent to hell, no one can rescue them. It's a done deal. For time without end. Captain Kirk, John Wayne, the Airborne Rangers—no one you can think of can help you out once you're there.

Do Nice People Really Go to Hell?

With all that he did for Spock we can conclude that Kirk believed some nice people go to hell. (Spock was nice and Kirk risked everything to save him.) But do they? The odds strongly shout "YES!"

The two movies gave us the false impression that all the rest of the characters were going to heaven. Only Spock appeared at risk. But Kirk, McCoy, Sulu, Uhura, Chekov, and Scotty were also nice people. So was Kirk's son. Weren't they in jeopardy of hell, too?

I think they were.

Do you know where you're going when you die? You're a nice person, aren't you? Do you think being nice will help your situation? Are you betting eternity on being nice enough?

The Baseball Hall-of-Famer Yogi Berra once said, "It ain't over 'til it's over." That statement may be true of a baseball game, but it's not true of life. Listen! If the Bible is right, it ain't over *when* it's over. Death only means life is over on this earth. But awareness continues someplace else. That makes life-and-death decisions "small potatoes." The more important consideration involves eternal life and eternal death because the end of physical life is just another beginning.

Physical life lasts only a lifetime. A soul last forever.
You don't want to spend forever in hell. Heaven is
the place to be.

Spock demonstrated the value of physical life and that nice people really do go to hell.

Kirk will show us the value of a soul.

We understand the occasional necessity to sacrifice one or a few lives to save many. As has been said, generals do it all the time. So do heroes. But sacrificing physical life to save a soul is a much bigger deal indeed. That's why Christ's death is so significant. One man gave his life to save the souls of all those who would follow him. He didn't die to save lives. He died to give eternal life to the souls of men and women and boys and girls.

The giving of lives whose souls are not in jeopardy of hell to rescue souls that are going there is far more important. Physical life has great value . . . but eternal life is worth infinitely more.

That's a weighty principle that the Bible confirms. Like I said, the story of the ninety-nine sheep and one is proof positive. In the next chapter we'll look at the value of that one stupid sheep that wanders off from the herd.

CHAPTER FOUR

A LESSON FROM CAPTAIN KIRK

(There is nothing more valuable than a soul.)

The needs of the one outweigh the needs of the many." When I heard that at the conclusion of "Star Trek III", I had a classic "Aha!" experience. It hit me like a ton of bricks. I finally understood the parable of the ninety-nine sheep and one:

> Suppose one of you has a hundred sheep and loses one of them. Does he not leave the ninety-nine in the open country and go after the lost sheep until he finds it? And when he finds it, he joyfully puts it on his shoulders and goes home. Then he calls his friends and neighbors together and says, 'Rejoice with me; I have found my lost sheep.' I tell you that in the same way there will be more rejoicing in heaven over one sinner who repents than over ninety-nine righteous persons who do not need to repent. (Luke 15:4-7)

I never understood why a responsible shepherd would put a whole herd at risk for one lousy sheep that didn't have sense enough to come in out of the rain. Don't waste your time looking for the lost one. Not if it puts the herd at risk. Rustlers and coyotes could have a field day with a herd left unattended. Maybe the stray will wander back, maybe not. Why gamble? The downside risk is too great for such a small upside potential. At least you still have ninety-nine.

But that's not the way God sees it. Not then, not now. God doesn't view the loss of the herd as downside risk at all. And he sees the upside as having the maximum return possible. Paul explained it this way:

> I eagerly expect and hope that I will in no way be ashamed, but will have sufficient courage so that now as always Christ will be exalted in my body, whether by life or by death. For to me, to live is Christ and to die is gain. If I am to go on living in the body, this will mean fruitful labor for me. Yet what shall I choose? I do not know! I am torn between the two: I desire to depart and be with Christ, which is better by far; but it is more necessary for you that I remain in the body. (Philippians 1:20-24)

What's the worst thing that can be done to a Christian? Kill him! But dying is a good thing because he will go to heaven and be with God. That was Paul's attitude and it eliminated fear.

The apostle said he was ready to die because he would really like to be with his Heavenly Father. But for the sake of the believers he would be content to live and continue ministering. He wins if he dies, and he wins if he lives. Not having a downside risk gives him a great outlook and total freedom. He doesn't own anything, so there is nothing to lose. And he doesn't even own his life any more. Paul has given it to the Lord. That doesn't matter, either.

So you see, there is no risk when the shepherd leaves the herd. The ninety-nine sheep were saved sheep and represent people who have a personal relationship with Christ. Christians, in the truest sense of the word. You can't do much to them. What matters is saving the lost one (the one going to hell) . . . even at the risk of losing part or all of the herd. It's the principle for missionaries.

Give one life to save several lives. That makes sense. But to give many lives whose souls are saved in order to save one lost soul makes even more sense. You see, the bigger issue is the soul, not the life.

> Life is temporal. A soul lasts forever. It's easy to see which is more important.
> A soul has the greater value.

Kirk understood. Not about Jesus or what he did. We can be pretty sure of that. But the captain did have a grasp of the importance of a soul. Spock showed us that the value of a life was one thing, but Kirk showed us that the value of a soul was quite another. The difference is the difference between chicken feathers and chicken salad . . . and that's a big difference. The point is, there is no comparison. A soul has the greater value.

Kirk valued Spock's soul.

How much?

The captain risked his career, court martial, and dishonor. We can conclude that Captain Kirk thought Mister Spock's soul was worth more than his own achievements. But he also risked his life and the life of his son. Remember, his son was killed. Can we conclude that the captain valued his Vulcan friend's soul more than life—even the life of his son? I think we can. Captain Kirk was willing to pay a great deal. Everything. It's impossible to draw any other conclusion. The captain believed Spock's soul to be worth more than anything he had to lose. You can tell that's true by what Kirk risked.

What would you pay for a soul? What would you risk? Do you understand the value of your soul? Is your soul at risk?

. . . Don't answer yet. You don't have enough information to decide. Before you can understand the value of a soul, you need to know what a life is worth.

The Rising Cost of Living

Environmental safety programs provide guidelines to the value of life. So do insurance companies and lawsuits. What we'll spend to save lives in the work place and what we're worth to our heirs in settlements after death will help establish our worth.

Our body chemicals were worth $7.28 in 1985.[27] (In that regard, I am probably worth more than you are. I'm 6'8" and weigh 230 pounds.) Life must be worth the difference between the value of our elements and what we are willing to spend to save it. Or life must be worth what we are willing to pay to compensate for its loss.

In America one way of determining the value of life is by calculating the number of work-related deaths recorded over a period of time, assessing the amount of money spent to improve the work environment or add safety factors on a job site, and then re-measuring work-related deaths over the same period of time. Divide the number of lives saved into the amount spent and we have the value of a life. Work-safety officials are currently spending as much as 3.5 million dollars per life saved. And the Environmental Protection Agency is spending from $400,000 to 7 million dollars per life saved, depending on the program.[28]

An insurance group put a housewife's value at 1.4 million dollars to show that she needed life insurance.[29] Some executives have been worth as much as 7 million dollars to their companies after courtroom litigation. In 1979 plane-crash victims averaged more than $500,000 in court-awarded compensation. That number is currently in the $350,000 range. We're not worth as much now if we crash in an airplane as we were if we had "bought the farm" in a plane fifteen years ago. Inflation has not increased the value of plane crash victims.

As Mister Spock would say, "Interesting!"

There have been times and places in human history when life wasn't worth much at all. Slavery, attempts to exterminate races, refusal to help starving masses, man's cruelty to the poor and underprivileged, sweat shops, "snuff" films, porn flicks, and abuse of children all demonstrate a low value of life. Baby girls in China have less value than baby boys. With the size of families being regulated, parents of girls will often kill their daughters until they have a boy. Life had little value in Cambodia during the "killing fields" years, and isn't worth much today in famine stricken-Africa. But your death is worth up to seven million dollars in the United States if you are a high-earner.

Are folks from different walks of life worth more than others? Are people who die one way worth more than if they die another? Is life in one country worth more than in another.

It looks like it.

Does that mean life is like any other commodity that has swings in value according to conditions in the marketplace?

Yes! There are value variables in man's determination of the worth of life. Let's look at a few of them.

Supply and Demand

In economics, value is primarily determined by supply and demand. The greater the supply, the less a commodity is worth. The greater the demand, the more people will pay for it. We value gold because it's pretty and rare. It's the same with diamonds. Other precious stones aren't perceived as being as attractive as diamonds. And other gems are easier to obtain. Diamonds are tough to find. The result: diamonds have greater value than other precious gems. Supply and demand dictate worth.

The same principles tend to apply to the value of life. Life isn't as precious in China and India. There are so many people, life has been devalued. When you couple large population with poverty and disease and then add a fatalistic religion, life's value further diminishes. Rats and cows are just as valuable as people in India. Starvation in Africa and death in Haiti is commonplace. Even in America's inner cities, kids will kill for a pair of sneakers—or a dirty look. Death has little meaning and life has little value in those places. We become immune because the masses involved are so great. Huge numbers make life too impersonal.

But strand a few whales in the ice pack in the Arctic, call attention to the situation with television coverage, and we'll spend millions to save them. Saving a few starving people when there are so many isn't news. But saving a few whales when there are so few is. Does that make whales more valuable than people?

Some people feel their pet is worth more than a starving child. I have a cat named Stephanie. For what it costs to feed her each month I could feed a starving child through Compassion (we do) or World Vision. What does that say about my values? I have but one cat, and I'm attached. I don't know any of the millions of starving kids.

This whole concept is getting scary. But you ain't heard nothin' yet.

How Much Does It Cost?

Supply and demand is one criterion for establishing value. Cost effectiveness is another. Try this on for size:

> Researchers from Brown University and a Rhode Island hospital did a cost-benefits analysis of treating handicapped infants. The answer: For birth weights of less than 900 grams, or about two pounds, costs per survivor exceeded the child's potential average lifetime earnings. Rescuing heavier babies returned more than the expense to society.[30]

Some people are suggesting that we make a person's earning potential the guideline for saving his or her life. Life and death decisions are being made on the basis of cost effectiveness.

Don't be shocked. People are doing that now in other ways. Some abortions are performed for economic reasons. If a mother can't afford a kid she can kill it, as long as it's in the womb. If she waits a day until the kid is in a crib, we'll call it murder. What a difference a day makes.

As we have seen, our society values life on the basis of supply and demand and cost effectiveness. People also value other people on the basis of relationship, how good or bad they've been, and their potential and productivity.

You've just jumped into a burning school bus. You have two arms to grab two kids and run before it blows. No second trips. Your son and daughter are in the second row. How do you choose who to take? Wouldn't you bypass those in the front seats to get to your kids? I would, too. Loved ones are worth more to us than people we don't know. So are good friends and some relatives.

Over the years I've asked people what their criteria would be if they would spend their money to save a life. In my informal study, relationship has been the most important criterion for establishing value. The second most often mentioned prioritizing factor pertained to the perceived goodness of that life. How good or bad has the person been in comparison with others?

Kind of Sin (how good or bad?)

If I'm going to spend some money, I want my dollars to count. Nobody likes a bad investment. That's why most people would rather spend their money on someone who is perceived to be a good person than on a bad one. I'd spend my money to save a white collar criminal before I would a murderer, wouldn't you? Give me a teller of lies over the "night stalker" any day. These days adulterers aren't considered criminals, so most people (including me) would spend their money faster for them than they would a rapist. Who would you choose between a skid row alcoholic or an outlaw? I'd spend my money on the drunk.

Then there are some of us who would rather just keep the money. You might think, I'm not interested in saving a serial killer who has no conscience. Let him burn. I could use a new car. I don't want to spend any money on a non-repentant chronic child molester. I'm afraid he'll do it again. Let him burn, too.

Baby needs a new pair of shoes! Are there circumstances that would cause me to value money over lives? It looks like it. And I'm embarrassed as I write. I must not have a thorough-enough understanding of the value of a soul.

In addition to the variables mentioned so far, there are two more that I'd like to discuss briefly. The first is potential and productivity. The second is religion.

Potential and Productivity

If the amount of money I have to spend on rescuing souls is fixed, I want to get as much bang for my buck as I can. I do like a bargain. So I think I would spend my money on someone who, in addition to being a good person, would also do the most good.

Let's assume I have a fixed amount of money. With it I can save the life of one more person. My choice must be made between you and the next Billy Graham. Guess what? Burn, baby, burn. Tough break. You're toast.

Wouldn't you spend more on Mother Teresa than some mean-mouth wife-beater? Me, too. And most would spend more on a young person who has his whole life in front of him than on an older person who has left most of his behind. Wouldn't you spend more on a healthy baby than one with defects? If you had to make the choice, sure. Unless it was yours, or unless the old person was your mom or dad.

Religion

As was previously stated, rats, cows, insects and humans all have the same value to a Hindu. Don't kill that rat. It might be your brother. The cow might be your uncle. And that ant might be your aunt. In India suffering is considered part of perfecting a person for their next life, so no one wants to help. Pain is seen as God's will.

Fatalistic religions devalue life.

Ron Carlson mentioned that during wars and after catastrophes you rarely see Hindus, Moslems or Buddhists caring for their fellow Hindus, Moslems or Buddhists. The group you'll see helping is the Red Cross.[31]

The red in the cross represents the blood of Christ. The cross represents how he died and why. And that symbol is internationally recognized as the sign of compassion and caring.

> Life is held in high esteem where Christianity has
> left its mark. Except to loved ones, it has little value
> where Jesus is not honored.

We have to conclude that the value of life depends on a multiple of variables. Supply and demand in the marketplace is one of them. Cost effectiveness, relationship, how good or bad, potential and productivity, and religion are others. The value of life certainly varies culturally as well.

These are a few of the variables that determine the value of a life. But what about a soul? Do the same variations in value apply?

The Value of a Soul

Remember the variables by which we determine the value of life? We use the same variables to determine the value of a soul, but an element of belief must be thrown in or we won't spend as much.

If you are in a burning car and I know you're about to lose your life, I'll probably react to save you. But I can't see your soul. And I don't know if you are going to hell, or even if there is such a place. I've never seen it. And you are such a nice person I can't imagine you ending up there anyhow. The result is that I won't risk as much to save your soul because I'm not sure of your outcome. In the burning car I know if you're going to die. I don't know if you are going to hell. If I'm going to risk something, it's easier to do it if I'm sure of the consequences. That's why I tend to risk more to save a life than a soul.

> A life is tangible and its loss directly impacts me. A soul is an intangible and its loss impacts God. Most people care more about themselves than God, so they care more about lives than souls.

This soul business requires an element of faith that the loss of life doesn't require. That's why most people will pay more for a life than a soul.

If we don't believe nice people really do go to hell, we're not going to risk much to save them. But if someone gave you this book they must value you greatly.

Our ways really are different from God's ways and our hearts are dissimilar indeed because none of our "value variables" alter the value of a soul in God's eyes. Let me show you what I mean.

No Variables with God

Are you worth less to God if you live in an overpopulated country?

Are you worth less if you are among the thousands who are starving?

Is your worth established by your economic contribution or cost?

Is your worth based upon your "closeness" to God?

Is your worth to God established by your circumstances or something you do or don't do?

Does Jesus sort out our value according to man's variables? Absolutely not!!! Does he play favorites, like we do? Not on your life! Perhaps I should say, "Not on your soul!" Matthew offers proof positive.

> While he was still speaking to the multitudes, behold, his mother and brothers were standing outside, seeking to speak to him. And someone said to him, 'Behold, Your mother and Your brothers are standing outside seeking to speak to You.' But he answered the one who was telling him and said, 'Who is My mother and who are My brothers?' And stretching out his hand toward his disciples, he said, 'Behold, My mother and My brothers! For whoever does the will of My Father who is in heaven, he is My brother and sister and mother.' (Matthew 12:46-50)

Jesus made two very important points in this passage. The first pertains to our relationship with him.

His critics thought he had just put down his mom.

"Mother hater! Mother hater! Jesus hates his mother," is what his detractors said about him.

But what he had just said was that blood-line relationships, as important as they are, end with the cessation of life. Spiritual relationships on the other hand last for all eternity, making them far more important indeed.

Jesus had also just said something about love. "God is love, you understand that," would be the beginning of his explanation if he were offering it today. "And I am God in flesh. Since God loves perfectly, I too love perfectly. I can only love the way God loves, because that's who I am. That makes me incapable of loving in degrees. Therefore, I cannot love my mother any more than I love you, nor you any more than my mother."

What an unbelievable revelation!

Jesus loves you just as much as his own mom.

WOW! No matter how unlovely you think you are, Jesus loves you as much as he does his mother. Your image of yourself doesn't alter his love for you one whit. If you are one of his followers you will not take your trip into the kingdom in "coach " or in the back of the bus. Those who know him will go "first class" all the way, regardless of their status in life. There is no caste system in the kingdom.

So what's your soul worth? What is its value? Well, let me tell you one thing. Your value has not been established by the variables of man. It doesn't vary according to market conditions. As a matter of fact there are no variables determining your worth from God's perspective. One act, and only one, determines the value of your soul. You are worth whatever the life of God's Son is worth to the his Father. And nothing else approaches that kind of value.

> You are the most valuable entity in the universe.

A Final Word about Relationship

The bottom line is that just as Jesus doesn't play favorites among those who know him; neither does our past get in the way of our personal relationship with him. That's good news. God does not love in degrees. He does not value one person more than another. So in that regard, relationship is not an issue. But relationship is an issue in that you must know Jesus Christ personally. His love for you won't alter, whether or not you enter into a relationship with God through Christ. His love for you isn't conditional. But the forgiveness of your sin is. You must have a relationship with Jesus Christ or you will receive the justice your sin demands. Any other conclusion is a long shot.

Do you have a deeper understanding of the value of a soul? I hope so. Now couple your understanding of value with the reality that nice people really do go to hell. Let them collide. If you do, your life will never be the same. How could it be?

Star Trek Debriefing—Stacking the Facts

What kind of friends did Spock have? They were very good friends indeed. Like the one who gave you this book.

How do we know? They risked everything, especially Captain Kirk. He believed Spock's soul was worth more than his son's life. Wow! It was a tough call, but he was right, assuming his son was somehow prevented from going to hell, too.

Is it worth risking everything to solve the problems of eternity for those around us? Kirk thought so, for his friend at least. He proved it by what he did.

Would he have done the same for one of the other members of the crew?

It depends. He wouldn't if he didn't value them sufficiently. And he wouldn't if he hadn't believed in the reality of hell and that nice people go there.

Would he have done it for somebody he didn't know?

Probably not. He's human and has the value variables of man, not God. Too bad.

But what if he was totally sold out to the reality of hell and thoroughly understood the value of a soul?

Then he would probably become a missionary, a pastor, a full-time preacher, go to Bible school—or more likely, stay right where he was in Star Fleet, doing what he was doing, and become an enthusiastic ambassador for Jesus Christ. That would be the response of a totally sold out, on fire, goin'-for-it, Jesus-lovin' believer.

Let's get down to brass tacks.

How did Spock know he would spend eternity in hell?

Tradition? Heritage? Family upbringing? A holy book? We

don't know everything. Ultimately I would assume it was faith. Unknowns have to be dealt with by faith.

You never have all the facts. Most decisions in life are made knowing only part of the story. There is almost always something more to be learned about everything. That's certainly true of religion.

So how did Captain Kirk come to believe Mister Spock was in hell?

He had to bridge the chasm of the unknown by faith. The rest of the crew did, too. But they didn't have to make the leap blindly. There was enough information to make an intelligent decision.

The events in Spock's circumstances played out one at a time, as most circumstances do. The result was a progressive stacking of singular facts. Solitary details are rarely enough to erase doubts. It's unusual when one piece of information proves or disproves anything. It's the stack that has to make sense. So Kirk was stuck with his doubts as the story unfolded.

But when the story was complete, and the facts had been compiled, there was enough information to intelligently draw a conclusion. Why? Because all the data was in harmony. When the facts at hand are not contradictory, you have convincing evidence that usually makes doubt go away. That's what happened for Kirk.

Here is how the facts of this story came together. It's a chronicle of the evolution of the captain's faith. I've included the thoughts he had with the revelation of each development.

Spock had always been reliable. But was the first officer operating with correct information? He might have been convinced of his religious belief—and been wrong. Lots of folks have been sincerely wrong. Kirk knew that.

Sarek, Spock's dad, was an Ambassador. His reputation was above reproach. That helped. But were the Vulcan traditions real or contrived? How objective can a person be when it comes to religion? Risking everything on the basis of some system of belief was asking a lot. I suspect the captain thought about that some too.

Dr. McCoy had added credibility—or had he? It was Spock who had implanted his convictions in the good doctor's head. So how much evidence had McCoy's testimony really provided after all? His was a most convincing argument, but it could have been wrong. If Spock was wrong, so was the doctor.

And how reliable were Kirk's own thoughts? Hearing Spock's voice in his head could have been a purely psychological manifestation. A feeling or an emotion is certainly not enough upon which to risk everything.

But the captain knew two Vulcans were saying that one of them was in hell. Kirk could not remember either of them ever being wrong. And since no Vulcan had ever lied in all of recorded history, that was pretty convincing evidence in itself, especially when all the other facts confirmed what they said to be true. Kirk had questioned every item of information, as any intelligent person would—and should. But when each piece of data confirmed all the other data, he could no longer substantiate his doubts. It's hard to stand firm against the harmony of the facts.

A compilation of independent sources with each piece being in harmony becomes a most convincing argument, especially when coupled with testimony from someone who has never told a lie. Captain Kirk didn't have all the facts, but considering the gravity of the situation, he felt he had enough. The captain chose to believe that nice people really do go to hell and that there is nothing more valuable than a soul. Spock was in trouble. Kirk and his friends had to do what they could to solve Spock's problem with hell.

One day you'll die. That's a fact. Do you have a potential problem with hell in your future? That's where a person has to face up to the consequences of a bad bet. It's a whole bunch better when you can look forward to heaven. That's where winners go. The existence of hell and heaven means death is not the end. It is really just a beginning. So let's talk about it.

Death! How fun!

CHAPTER FIVE

WHY DREAD DEATH?

(Most people lose the bet.)

Nothing is as sure as death and taxes, that's what they say. Well, I don't know who "they" are, but they're wrong. I know people who don't pay taxes. But there is one thing that's for sure. Death! And I don't personally know anyone who either hasn't had to or who won't have to die. Do you?

Death is something we'll all do, and it's scary. Why? What's next is an unknown. That's why.

The unknown is a scary place. It's why I step on spiders. *I'm afraid of you.* Smoosh!

Isn't it the same for you?

We tend to avoid situations where we don't know the outcome. The unknown is disconcerting and we become fearful. It's almost a universal truth. Of course there are a few who thrive on the exhilaration of the unfamiliar. The ones who like to walk on the edge. Rock climbers, sky divers and bungee jumpers are all in that category. But remember, even daredevils are aware of their odds and the probabilities of survival. They rarely spend much time thinking about the possibilities of death, because they aren't doing it to die. The event is for fun. But death is the one unknown that brings fear into even the most courageous of characters. Look into a daredevil's eyes after one of his friends has died. You'll see fear lurking there.

Death: the Ultimate Unknown

A great rabbi was on his deathbed in the final minutes of his life. "How do you feel?" was his son's concerned question.

"How do you think I feel?" was the old man's frightened reply. "I'm about to find out if what I've believed all my life is true." The man was afraid. Death can do that to a person.

Have you ever seen a dead body? My first encounter came when I was in sixth grade. My dad and I were in the High Sierras doing some fishing for golden trout. We had come into the high country via a light airplane. The landing strip was noted to be very difficult and wasn't a place for beginners.

Later the next day a plane tried to land, but it came in too high and too fast. The pilot flew out the end of canyon, circled all the way around and tried again fifteen minutes later (it took that long to make the circle). Same problem. He was too high. But instead of flying all the way around, he turned around in the wide end of the canyon and flew back trying to land from the wrong direction. Again he overshot the runway, only this time he flew into the narrow, steep-walled, box canyon from which there was no way out.

Tiny, the three-hundred-pound camp caretaker, hollered, "Get the buckets and the shovels. I've never seen anyone make it out of there yet."

As I watched, the plane went to the far right of the canyon wall, utilizing all the space it could, did a hard turn to the left, but stalled and did a wing-over into a large pine tree. Fire and smoke were instantaneous. Within minutes we were on our way to fight fire.

When we got there I could only see two dark, dead shapes. One in the wreckage in the midst of the fire, the other off to the side. I was on the water detail.

After lots of thoughts and very little sleep, my dad and I had the morning watch until the coroner arrived. There was a tarp with two shapes under it. I walked by several times, looking and wondering. My father finally said, "You'll have to face death sometime. If you want to face it now, we'll do it together. If you want to wait, that's fine too. It's your call."

Death is such a scary thing. It took another half hour for me to make up my mind. Dad pulled back the corner of the covering and I saw the great fear-maker for the first time. Death and I had looked at each other face to face.

Have you looked death in the eye?

The Harsh Reality of It All

Some people say dying won't be so bad—it's how you die that's scary. But I don't know if that's true. When you take a corner too fast in a car, what happens to your stomach? It flip-flops. Why? Death is a frightening prospect. When you're alone in your house at night and hear "that sound," why does the adrenaline shoot through your body? Because you are scared out of your gourd. Why? Death is scary. You may tell me or yourself you're not afraid of death, but your stomach will give you away every time.

If the *possibility* of death scares you, deep down what must the *inevitability* of it do to you?

Dying is unavoidable and it's scary. However, what the Bible says about death can be reassuring—if you're on the way to paradise.

I love the way the Apostle Paul faced death. The Romans imprisoned him and threatened, "We're gonna' kill ya'."

"Great!" hollered Paul. "I'll be with the Lord in paradise."

"Well, since you want that, we're not gonna' do it. Nope,

we're gonna' torture you instead. Whadda' ya' think of that, wise guy?"

"Wonderful, I'll identify with the sufferings of my Lord. Just be creative."

Perplexed, they threatened to chain him to a guard and rotate the jailer every four hours.

"That's the best yet," was Paul's ecstatic reply. "What a great witnessing opportunity. It takes me about that long to thoroughly explain how to be born again."

What do you do to a guy like that? Anything? Nothing? The Romans couldn't figure it out, either. Paul was ready for death. You can be too . . . unless you are planning on beating the odds.

What Are Your Odds of Not Dying?

Name two Old Testament characters who never had to die. If you said "Enoch and Elijah" you have been raised in Sunday school. Only these two excaped death.

What are your odds of being like Enoch and Elijah? Not very good, are they? So you might as well face it. Death is going to be a reality for you.

But what happens next? Billy Graham said, "It becomes increasingly evident that the way we view death determines, to a surprising degree, the way we live our lives."[32]

If you believe existence ceases with death, you might as well get all the gusto you can get in this life, since you only go around once.

If you believe in reincarnation, you won't be that worried about the here and now because you think you can keep going around again and again until you get it right.

If you believe hell is spent on earth while you're here, your behavior may not be impacted much.

But if you believe in the heaven and hell of the Bible, you'll live your life in the light of heaven and tell your friends about the awfulness of hell.

Actually, if the Bible is correct, it won't matter what anybody thinks or how they believe. If the whole Christian deal is real, the opinions, philosophies, and religions of men and women won't amount to a hill of beans. Truth is all that will count. Whoever is right will win. Those who are wrong will lose big time. The winners will have a memorial service. The losers will have a funeral.

A Funeral or a Memorial Service

When you choose to trust Christ your belief takes the sting out of death. It makes a memorial service out of a funeral. I talked about it in one of my newsletters:

A funeral or a memorial service? A rose by any other name. A loved one is gone and I am left with a hole in my being, a void in my soul . . . an emptiness in my gut. I know, I know! Don't preach to me. Christ will fill me with Himself, but that will take time. Right now I hurt like crazy. I cannot be comforted.

A funeral or a memorial service? They're for the survivors—the ones who remain, like me. I've lost a loved one and I need to be propped up. And I've been reminded of my mortality, of how temporal I am. I really am "just passin' through." I'm terminal. I just don't know what's going to kill me—yet. It's a tough reality. Don't remind me. This event reminds me. I guess that's good.

A funeral or a memorial service? When the deceased is a believer I should be joyful. If I really believe, I am convinced the departed is in the presence of the Lord. The problem is that I am selfish and I'm sad about my loss more than I am joyous for my loved one's new situation. You can measure my depth of belief by my joy or sorrow. Or was it selfishness? Or grief? At a time like this, who cares?

A funeral or a memorial service? If the deceased is a nonbeliever there can be no joy. At least not for the believers attending. A funeral for the lost is a tragic event. Hell is an impossible concept of absolute truth. Sobering. And no amount of fluff from a pulpit can offset that reality. Nonbelieving attendees sit in their confusion and try to make sense of life, but life doesn't make sense apart from Christ. A Christian knows what really happens. Oh the tragedy! Oh the pain!

A funeral or a memorial service? I think it's an event that should be used as the departed's last chance to witness. If a funeral isn't evangelistic, a tremendous opportunity has been lost. It should be a time to let a Christian's life speak through their death. And these events are an advertisement for Christ. People who don't know him are susceptible to the way believers handle deep personal loss. And non-believers will go to say good-bye when they wouldn't darken the door of a church for any other occasion. Yes, the gospel should be preached.

A funeral or a memorial service? Too often it's a time to say things about people that should have been said when they were alive. I'm reminded of a story about a raccoon and a porcupine. It's hard to get close to a porcupine. The raccoon had been shot and was blind. The porcupine took care of the raccoon until it died. But the porcupine failed to say how he felt about the raccoon. After all, the porcupine had never been close to anyone before. But as he spoke the words to the raccoon's dead body the porcupine wished he hadn't waited so long, because he realized how empty words that cannot be heard really are. It's a shame to have to say things to a dead body that should have been said in life.

A funeral or a memorial service? It's an opportunity to support and prop up the bereaved, a recognition and reminder of our mortality, a gut check for selfishness and love, a time to grieve, a proclamation of mission and life's purpose, and a chance to get a few things off our chests. But the words aren't synonyms.

Funerals are final. Memorial services are more like "see ya' later." The lost have funerals. The saved remember those who are with the Lord until they join them.

I pray that your loved ones have a memorial service for you and that you won't be having a funeral.

Sooner or later you will die and someone will probably bury your old body. The Bible says that just happens once. "Man is destined to die once, and after that to face judgment." (Hebrews 9:27) There are a few in the Bible who died twice. And people today report having died and returned. I don't know about out-of-body experiences, a long tunnel and the bright light many report having seen. All I know is that unless God chooses to make an exception we are only going to die once.

Can God make exceptions to his rules?

Sure!

Why?

Because he's God.

But that might not be the reason in this case, because there are different kinds of death. Actually there are three. And if you are one kind of dead when you die, you'll spend forever dead.

Confused? Stay tuned. Let me explain.

What Kind of Dead Are You?

We've talked about the inevitability of death and the fear associated with dying. But we talked about death in one-dimensional terms. Death is really three-dimensional: physical, spiritual, and eternal. Each is mentioned in the Bible where Jesus is speaking to a woman named Martha:

> I am the resurrection and the life; he who believes in Me shall live, even if he dies, and everyone who lives and believes in Me shall not die. Do you believe this? (John 11:25–26)

That's a tough passage, but look closely. You'll find three kinds of death wrapped up in the verse. Keep in mind that each kind of death has a corresponding life. Let me add some extra terms to show you what I mean:

> I am the resurrection and the life; he who believes (spiritual death to spiritual life) in Me shall live (eternal life instead of eternal death) even if he dies (physical life to physical death), and everyone who lives (who is physically alive) and believes in Me (spiritual death to spiritual life) shall never die (eternal life not eternal death). Do you believe this?

Death was not in God's original plan. It came with Adam and Eve's rebellion—in all three forms, physical, spiritual and eternal. Illness wasn't a part of the deal called life either. But since the days in the Garden of Eden, bodies that weren't supposed to get sick, age or die, do—making physical death a reality. Babies have been born spiritually dead ever since (I'll tell you about that in a minute). All those who haven't solved their spiritual problem before physical death occurs are left in big trouble.

They're in a pickle because what happens next is eternal death.

Each kind of death is different from the others, but all are interrelated. It's important to understand this interrelationship. If you're confused, relax. I'll explain in more depth. We'll start with physical death.

Physical Death

The first kind of death is physical death. The Bible says death occurs when your spirit, whatever it is and wherever it is, leaves your body (James 2:26). When your conscious awareness, your soul—the entity or energy that is you—leaves the house you call your body, physical death occurs. What I am defining as physical death is different from the medical definition. Medical folks call you dead when your brain's waves flatten out and there is an irreversible loss of vital functions.

Apparently when Elijah, Jesus, Peter, and others raised people from the dead, those raised were medically dead, but their souls hadn't left yet. They must not have been biblically dead.

I don't know if any of the resurrection encounters in the Bible involved people whose souls had left their bodies or not. I don't think so because the verse in Hebrews says that happens only once. But Lazarus was non-functional and medically dead for almost four days, so we have to assume he was as dead as a person could be. Did his spirit leave his body? Who knows? And I don't know about the current rash of folks who have supposedly died on hospital operating tables and come back to life. Most, if not all, were likely to have been medically dead—not biblically dead (their souls hadn't left). Remember, if there are exceptions, they are not the rule. The rule is, "man is destined to die once, and after that to face judgment." The statement applies to women, too.

Physical death is a reality all of us will have to face, both with those near and dear to us, and personally. My mom died, my dad will, my wife, my kids and their kids will also. You will. Me, too. A person ought to be ready.

It's true that death can sometimes be postponed. I try to stay in pretty good shape by working out five times a week. My heartbeat is in the mid-fifties. My blood pressure is 110 over 70. My cholesterol is 176. I had a stress test and the doctor was impressed. We concluded that I am going to die healthier!

Death for me is getting closer, just as it is for you. That's when we'll be confronted with forever.

> When physical death occurs you can't kill the energy or entity that is you. You'll just relocate—to a place called eternity.

But *where* in eternity depends on whether or not you are still spiritually dead.

Spiritual Death

The second kind of "being dead" is spiritual death. Surprisingly enough, you were born that way. It's part of the consequence of original sin. Adam's sin infected you through your dad. He got it from his father, and so on—all the way back to Adam. It's called a sin nature (some people call it flesh) . . . and everybody's got one.

My daughter's name is Kim. This incident occurred when she was around nine months old.

My little girl couldn't quite walk yet, but she loved to hang onto furniture to get around. We had a low-profile stereo that had sliding doors in its top. Kim thought it was fun to slide the doors back and reach in. There was some good stuff to play with in there, like a clicker thing. And when she clicked it a wheel began to spin and an arm went back and forth and up and down too. What fun it was to make the wheel spin faster with her hand. Sometimes she liked to make it spin the other direction. Oh yes, Kim also loved to grab the moving arm and yank it back and forth and up and down. Consequently, the stereo became a no-no. I can't tell you how many times I had to reinforce the concept of no with Kim. And each time I said it, she became ever more defiant.

On the twenty-first go-round, Kim's whole disposition changed. Her demeanor altered. She thrust her face into my face, grimaced with the most defiant look she could muster, and thrust her hand back into the stereo, while glaring directly into my eyes. If that little girl could have spoken the words she would have said, "Bite the wall, Dad! Hang it in your ear, Pop! I'm gonna' do what I wanna' do, because I wanna' do it." I couldn't believe it. I was having a real confrontation with a nine-month-old kid.

I'm big, tall, ugly and have a deep voice. Listen, I'm intimidating. I can be a scary guy, but that little nine-month-old kid wasn't afraid.

I did realize I was in a battle and that if I lost the war the house would be run by a tiny tyrant.

Kim just glared, burning holes in me with her eyes as she started to thrust her hand back in. But then she paused, folded her arms, exhaled through her nose, turned and made her way to the other side of the room. It was over, but it had been quite a battle.

Now here's the question. Where did she get that?

I know! I know! From me. Right? You bet.

Hey, did your folks have to teach you to be disobedient? No! You picked it up naturally. And that's the point.

Have you ever seen little kids play with each other? They're vicious. "Gimmee!" and "Mine!" are shouts that are accompanied with eye gouges and face scratching. The only time rug rats are sweet is when they're asleep. You see, they have a sin nature . . . and so do you. You were born separated from God. You were born in sin . . . Adam's (Psalm 51:5). You got a sin nature and you got it from your dad (Exodus 20:5). You need to face it—you were born spiritually dead.

The Bible says we're either children of God or children of the devil (1 John 3:10). Now don't get upset. Cool your jets. If you aren't a Christian in the truest sense of the word (some people call themselves Christians who are still spiritually dead), I didn't just call you a devil worshipper or a dirty, rotten person. Nor did I defame your character. That verse refers to ownership. Either God owns you or the devil does. It refers to with whom you'll spend eternity. You are either spiritually alive or you're spiritually dead. But changing your status is your call. No one can do it for you, and it doesn't happen by being good.

Spiritual birth requires a decision. Spiritual deadness doesn't. As a matter of fact, no decision on the matter is considered a decision in opposition to God's solution and leaves a person spiritually dead. That's why no bet is still a bet. Interestingly enough, "no call" is the decision most people will make. Matthew 7:14-15 confirms it. More people will choose hell than heaven:

> Enter through the narrow gate. For wide is the gate and broad is the road that leads to destruction, and *many* enter through it. But small is the gate and narrow the road that leads to life, and only a *few* find it (Matthew 7:13–14) [emphasis mine].

I'm convinced babies and children go to heaven. David told us he would be with his baby in paradise and Jesus never condemns children. But they are born spiritually dead, separated from God, and at some point in time become accountable for their sin (if you can read this book you are accountable). Although most people won't choose it, the Bible offers only one solution for the condition. It's called spiritual birth.

Spiritual birth occurs through Jesus Christ. Christ is the only way to solve the problem of spiritual deadness. He personally said so: "I am the way and the truth and the life. No one comes to the Father except through me" (John 14:6). God doesn't mention any other method. Jesus called it being "born again".

> In reply Jesus declared, 'I tell you the truth, no one can see the kingdom of God unless he is born again.'
> 'How can a man be born when he is old?' Nicodemus asked. 'Surely he cannot enter a second time into his mother's womb to be born!'
> Jesus answered, 'I tell you the truth, no one can enter the kingdom of God unless he is born of water and the Spirit. Flesh gives birth to flesh, but the Spirit gives birth to spirit. You should not be surprised at my saying, "You must be born again."' (John 3: 3–7)

We were born once physically. We're here. Another birth is necessary. Not a second physical birth. Rather, a spiritual one. It's crystal clear. The only solution to spiritual death is spiritual birth. And spiritual birth can only take place through Jesus Christ. God said so.

Physical death is unavoidable and ultimately out of your control. As I've said, you can delay it some, but you won't escape it. Eternity is also unavoidable and out of your control. You will spend it someplace, like it or not. However that is not true of being spiritually dead. You have the say-so in staying that way.

Here is an interesting thought. We make a big deal out of suicide, and I think we are correct to do so. Suicide should be against the law. Life is too precious to throw away. Yet, we don't make much of a fuss about folks who commit spiritual suicide. What does that say about our concept of the value of a soul?

Spiritual suicide is hearing the truth about Jesus Christ and not responding to it. If the Bible is right, people who reject the Son of God literally condemn themselves to hell. So don't wait too long to make your decision if you haven't already, because if physical death catches you spiritually dead, you're in the biggest trouble imaginable. You'll be a real hurtin' unit forever—because you'll have to endure eternal death.

Eternal Death

Eternal death is final, absolute, non-reversible, and lasts forever. It is spent wherever, in whatever, hell is. (Hell will be discussed thoroughly in the next chapter. Right now we'll concentrate on eternity.)

Eternity is a difficult concept to illustrate, but here goes anyhow. Some have suggested a bird relocating every grain of sand on the earth, but that doesn't quite do it unless you never let him stop. Although there are a lot of grains of sand, there are just so many. Grains of sand are finite. So that illustration doesn't work.

How about getting on a plane going west and continuing until you're east? Sounds like a dog chasing its tail. You would never arrive. But you would always know how long you have been traveling because you would be aware of time.

Some people don't like that illustration because they see eternity as being without time. It may be that there will be no time in the new heaven and the new earth. God created time; he can eliminate it if he wants to.

It's interesting that time isn't a constant. Scientists have discovered that people in the mountains live longer than those at sea level. It seems that those closer to sources of gravity age faster than those farther away. Therefore time goes slower out in space than it does on earth. That's one of the reasons why after a trip the space travelers are younger than their friends who were confined to the planet. However, there is another reason for the difference, and the concept offers some interesting possibilities regarding eternity.

The theory of relativity makes time relative to motion. The faster we travel the more time is compressed. For example, traveling at 160,000 miles per second for ten years in space equals twenty years on earth. But 170,000 miles per second for a day equals twenty years on earth. Einstein postulates that at the speed of light (186,000 miles per second) all time exists in the present.[33] Maybe that's how God can say the equivalent of, "I never was, I never will be. I AM!" If in heaven all time exists in the present, we who go there will not be bound by time either. But I doubt that the same will be true in hell. Hell might be a place where time stands still.

We are terrestrial creatures, so we will get new bodies. That means there will probably be gravity in heaven. But maybe not. There is a relationship between aging and gravity. Since we know that in heaven we won't age, gravity might not exist. If hell is in the center of the earth or in a black hole in space where gravity is infinitely concentrated, perhaps a person who is there will age forever—if that's possible.

Whew! That kind of thinking hurts my mind. Here's a thought about eternity that's more my speed. I was lighting my fireplace using a built in gas "cheater." Having turned on the gas, I stuck in a lighted match, but the gas jet blew out the flame. So, without turning off the gas, I fumbled around for another match, lit it and thrust it into the opening. What do you think happened? Sure, a big "pooooof" made all the hair disappear from the back of my hand. All I had left were those curly, smelly little "nubbins."

As I looked at the flames I thought about the times I've passed my finger through a candle's flame. Almost everyone has done that at some point in life. I decided I would do the same thing with the flame in the fireplace. Looking around to see if anyone was looking (I didn't want someone to see a grown man doing such a thing) I passed my hand quickly through the fire. It was so fun I did it a second time. Then I decided to put my hand in and leave it for ten seconds, just to see what would happen.

Stop what you're doing for a moment and look at a clock or

a watch and count out ten seconds. (At least do "one-thousand-one, one-thousand-two," etc. Do it. You'll miss the whole point if you don't.)

Under some circumstances ten seconds goes by rather quickly, but under those conditions it would be a long period of time, wouldn't it? I thought so, too, so I didn't put my hand in.

What if you put your hand in and left it for a minute? That would be a long minute.

How about an hour, and for some reason the hand wasn't consumed. Would it be a long hour? You bet!

How about a year, or a lifetime, or a really long time, like umpteen-jillion-quadtrillion-nonillion-decillion-billion years? Now that would be a long time in the fire.

Eternity is undoubtedly multi-dimensional, but since I'm an old athlete, and since old "jocks" aren't very smart, let's study eternity as a one-dimensional term. A line is one dimensional so that's what we'll use for our illustration.

Look to your left and imagine a clothes line running as far as your eye can see. If you're in a room, imagine the line running out through the wall. Have the line run right under your nose so that you have to look cross-eyed to see it. Now look to your right and see it going as far as your eye can see. To the left is eternity past, to the right is eternity future.

Let's plot some times on the eternal line. Using an ultra-fine-point accountant's pen, put a dot on the line right in front of your nose to represent ten seconds. Next, plot one minute. It's a dot, too. An hour, a year and a lifetime are also dots on the line. And get this, umpteen-jillion-quadtrillion-nonillion-decillion-billion years is also no bigger than a dot. All the dots are the same size because the ultra-fine-point pen is the only thing we have with which to mark. Actually, any whole number (not pi, which is an infinite number) will appear as a dot because the line is so long.

Can you imagine umpteen-jillion-quadtrillion-nonillion-decillion-billion years and have it only be a dot on a line that goes on forever? Try to grasp how long eternity is? It's tough because we're bound by our measurements of time.

Take one more step. Try to imagine spending forever, not with just your hand in a flame, but with your body totally immersed, experiencing the agony and yet never being consumed? That's the literal interpretation of what the Bible calls hell, and most people have a lot of trouble accepting that. If you are a skeptic, pay close attention to the next paragraph.

Keep in mind that illustrations rarely live up to the reality of what they are attempting to portray. A depiction is usually something *less* than the original. A copy of a video isn't as good as the original. It's true of a lithograph as well. Analogy works the same way. The real thing is better than a picture. Therefore, hell should be worse than any illustration we can dream up to describe it.

If the hell of the Bible is not literal fire, the real hell will be worse than our description of it.

Bingo! Lord, you got my attention with that revelation.

Mick Jagger, who is the lead singer for the Rolling Stones, has made reference on several occasions to having made a deal with the devil. Mick gave his soul in exchange for all the world has to offer. I wonder how he will feel about the length of his lifetime after he gets to compare it with the enormity of eternity. The former is a snap of the fingers. The latter is a timeless forever.

I'm trying to warn you about hell. My limitations as a writer keep me from doing a better job. And I don't know how to make you more aware of what eternity really is. I've tried. But heaven, hell, and forever are biblical concepts. Whether you end up in heaven or hell, you will remain there in a state of awareness forever, and it will be by your choice.

I believe the whole deal is real. Since I value you, my part is to make sure you hear the truth. Your part is to respond. That makes the next move yours.

Someone said, "Man's greatest need is to know what is his greatest need." The most important of life's decisions revolves around spiritual life and spiritual death.

> Being spiritually alive or spiritually dead at the time of physical death is the sole determiner of eternal life or eternal death.

Life poses no situation that has graver consequences. No dilemma you'll ever face rivals this one in importance.

Eternity hangs in the balance of your choice—your forever will be spent in either hell or heaven. We'll talk about both places in the next two chapters.

CHAPTER SIX

HELL
(Downside risk.)

The concept of eternity is true of every society ever studied. Only those few who stifle the still small voice of God and deny his existence don't recognize the existence of a forever somewhere. However, regardless of the mental gymnastics of the ones who deny God, when they stand before him they will be without excuse because God has planted the awareness of himself in the hearts of all people. (See appendix for detail on this concept.)

It still amazes me how those who reject the reality of their Heavenly Father cry out, "Oh my God," or "God help me," when they are surprised, scared or in "deep weeds." When it gets down to "brass tacks," we tend to cut through all the fluff and rhetoric. That's when most atheists admit their awareness of him.

It's interesting that when Gorbachev, an atheist, was being arrested by the perpetrators of the failed coup in August, 1991, he didn't tell them to go to Siberia, he told them to go to hell. Tell me, is Gorbachev really an atheist?

The rest of humanity is aware of God, although it's true that some just acknowledge him and love themselves. But even with inappropriate worship, intuitively most of us are aware that we continue on as an entity after we leave our earthly house. Eternity as a universal concept in societies around the world is one of the proofs of its reality.

You are intuitively aware of the reality of eternity, so proving it is probably not a big deal to you. You probably don't have to be persuaded about its existence. But where you spend it ought to get your interest. The Bible makes us aware of our need for concern.

Is the Bible God's revealed word to humankind? Yes or no? Which do you believe?

If you believe the Bible, it is impossible to read the book without realizing that eternity is spent in one of two places—heaven or hell. No other possibilities are offered. No other options really exist.

Assuming you believe the Bible, are you aware that the basic theme of the Old Testament is the promised coming of a Savior, and that the New Testament is about the fulfillment of that promise through Jesus Christ? Since Christ is the central focus of the Christian faith, you'd think that what he had to say was very important, wouldn't you? It is!

Try this on for size. Jesus said more about hell than he did about love, and he spoke of hell more than all the rest of the biblical preachers combined. Hell occupied his subject matter two-thirds more than heaven did.

Hell is real, my friend. Jesus said so—and it's the ultimate in scary thoughts.

Are you thinking, *Jay, are you trying to scare me?*

My answer, "You bet!"

It'll Scare the Heaven into You

Going into a battle during Desert Storm an officer hollered to his troops, "Give 'em hell!"

I'm hollering in this book, "Give 'em heaven!" Through the working of the Holy Spirit of God, I'd like to scare the heaven into you—and the hell right out.

Does the use of fear as a motivator bother you? Is the use of terror as a method to get your attention upsetting? Here's what one psychologist says about its use:

> When fear is used to motivate people, especially sensitive children, in the name of God, it is a grave mistake and constitutes one of the biggest dangers and difficult obstacles that young people have to overcome in order to live happy, fruitful, adult Christian lives.[34]

That's one side of the coin. Here is the other:

> If men do not fear the terror of the Lord they must experience that terror. *If you are not afraid of hell, you are almost certainly going there.*[35]
>
> Why, then, do so many vehemently oppose frightening children? They don't. They scare children away from fire, from electric sockets, from poisonous drinks or pills, from snakes, from certain toys, from anything that threatens them.
>
> Why, then, do almost all seem to oppose frightening children with hell? The answer is obvious: they wrongly fancy that children are not in danger of hell. *Can you imagine that a mother who would give her own life to save her child's wouldn't do everything to save her child from hell if she knew there was any danger?*[36]
>
> Why scare preaching? Two reasons: (1) God, in his Word, is a Scare Preacher; (2) The fear of hell is the only thing most likely to get worldly people thinking about the Kingdom of God. *No rational human being can be convinced that he is in imminent danger of everlasting torment and do nothing about it. But, you say, there are many now who fear hell, or say they do, and yet don't believe or seek the gift of faith. That is true, but, as we say, that only proves that they are no longer 'rational human beings'.*[37]

There is no question that some over-zealous preachers have done an overkill on hellfire and brimstone in the past. But "turn or burn, flip or fry, change your stroke or go down in smoke" kind of preaching has become a thing of the past. Some folks have been asking, "Whatever happened to the 'H' word?" This book is my response.

Is there a place for fear preaching? I think so. The Bible makes it clear that fear is a legitimate reason for coming to Christ. Granted, it is not the most desirable, virtuous, or noble of reasons. But it is a reason. Jesus made that clear.

He also preached rewards. Heaven later. And love, joy, peace, and all the rest of what's promised can be enjoyed now. Although it seems selfish, what I can get out of a right relationship with Christ is a legitimate reason for considering him. Whether it is a better reason than fear, I'm not prepared to say. I think so, but I'm not sure.

Of course, the most noble of reasons and the purest is the response of a grateful heart. When we understand what Christ did for us by taking the sins of mankind on his shoulders, our response should be gratitude and worship. When we put the price (Christ's death) and the payoff (overcoming the justice of hell and spending forever with God) together, can we respond any way other than with thankfulness?

All three reasons are biblically sound, regardless of the psychologist's warning. Perhaps Christ's use of fear and rewards are a way to get our attention. And then, once having gotten it, he processes us to the stage of gratefulness. Maybe the order ought to be reversed. Maybe we first ought to tell people about the love of God. If that doesn't work, then tell them what they can get out of a walk with Christ. If that doesn't do it, then, if they'll listen, resort to scaring the hell out of them, and replace it with the heaven that comes through a right relationship with Jesus Christ.

I don't know for sure. But this I do know.

> Jesus Christ used fear as a way to communicate the
> seriousness of the issue of hell.

Are you afraid of hell? If you're not "right in Christ," you should be.

Funny thing about fear. We hate it. That's why we tend to deny those things that cause us to be afraid. And—interestingly enough—when it comes to hell, most people are in a state of denial.

It's Hard to Believe

George Gallup, Jr. has compiled a variety of data in his fascinating book *The People's Religion: American Faith in the '90s*.[38] So have Patterson and Kim in their tacky 1991 release.

> 94 percent of the American population
>   believe in God.
>
> 81 percent believe in Judgment Day.
>
> 81 percent of the religiously active
>   believe in life after death
>
> 50 percent of the non-religiously active
>   believe in life after death
>
> 32 percent of the non-religiously active
>   do not believe in life after.
>
> 66 percent believe in heaven.
>
> 46 percent expect to spend eternity in heaven.
>
> 53 percent believe in hell.
>
> 4 percent expect to spend eternity in hell.

Only 4 percent of the American population believe they are going to hell. That is the most staggering statistic of all—for two reasons: (1) that so few see it as a real risk to be dealt with, and (2) that even 4 percent would be content to go there without doing something about it.

Why the dramatic differences between heaven and hell?

Denial!

Billy Graham in his book on death concluded, "Gallup surmises, and I tend to agree, that some of the reasons why more people believe in heaven than in hell is that 'Hell is like death—people try not to think about it.'" [39]

That's bizarre. It's the ultimate in a supernatural ostrich syndrome. Both concepts (heaven and hell) come from the same source (the Bible), but we mortals buy into one while denying the other, thinking belief will change reality. It's not rational, but it's the way most people deal with hell.

Denial, when coupled with our natural compassion and fear, produces a hope that hell will be something less than the Bible says it will be, including something less than eternal. We can't understand how a loving God can allow such a place, so we develop concepts such as purgatory (going to a hell-like place for a period of time, depending on how bad you've been), and paying penance (it's hard to believe that Christ paid our entire debt on the Cross, so we tend to think that more must be done, and we should be the ones to do it). Our conclusion is that if hell is for real, only really bad people go there (like in the movie Ghost where one of two nice people who are living together is murdered. The murderers went to hell. The guy who wasn't married to the girl he was living with went to heaven. Hollywood said that murder is bad; adultery is not—but that's not the way God sees it.)

If there is a hell, some folks would agree that murderers ought to go there, along with child molesters and drug pushers.

But there is a rather large group that believes that everyone ends up in heaven.

Everybody Goes to Heaven

Some of the most subtle forms of denial show up in doctrine that waters down the Bible. It's an attempt to get everyone into heaven and everybody out of hell.

Some believe there is no hell, only heaven. Others believe hell is spent on earth and we all go to heaven. Or if there is a purgatory, we all end up in paradise in the end, after we have paid penance for our sins. These ideas are called universalism, but there is no biblical support for the concept. The Scriptures have to be twisted way too much to make them even suggest the possibility.

Universalism is a non-biblical way for people to cope with their fear of hell. It is an escapist philosophy. Pure denial. So don't get sucked in. Mental gymnastics don't alter biblical truth, not if the whole deal is real. They didn't for Spock. They won't for you. Everybody will not end up in heaven. As a matter of fact, if the whole deal is real, most won't (Matthew 7:13–14). As I've pointed out, Jesus said so at the end of the Sermon on the Mount.

Contrary to what Christ said, George Gallup's numbers confirm that most people believe that hell is not a forever kind of place. The concept of annihilation is the result.

Nobody Goes to Hell

There are some high-powered theologians[40] who subscribe to the hope that those who go to hell just end as an entity. It's called annihilation. Eternal punishment is not a part of this idea. An individual has no awareness or existence. The person just ceases to be.

Consider this thought as an answer to annihilation:

Justice demands adequate punishment. Since punishment itself never produces repentance, justice requires it to go on forever. Even the very expression, "the annihilation of the wicked," is an outrage against justice, because sin requires punishment, not non-punishment which non-existence certainly is.[41]

Hell is a real deal and it doesn't end for anybody who's there. It can't because the same New Testament Greek and Hebrew words that describe the length of heaven are used to describe the length of hell. The wording of the Bible demands that one place last as long as the other, and that people in one location are just as aware for just as long as those in the other. Since God lives in heaven, having hell end would mean the end of heaven, and that kind of thinking would consummate in the extinction of God. Since God is eternal, heaven is eternal. And since heaven is eternal, hell must be, too. Since heaven will last forever, those who go there will enjoy it eternally. The same also has to be true of hell, only it's not enjoyed. Those who go to hell will suffer forever because that's how long it lasts. The Bible cannot be manipulated around that probability.

The Word of God says the smoke of hell will go up forever and ever. Revelation 14:11 states, "And the smoke of their torment rises for ever and ever." Mark 9:43 says hell is a place "where the fire never goes out." Since there are a finite number of people, if annihilation is correct, ultimately hell would run out of fuel. No fuel, no fire. No people means no smoke. No! Folks aren't fuel. People aren't consumed. The fires of hell are fueled by the justice of God, not what is thrown into them.

Hell is a beginning, not an end. It is the beginning of
an eternal state of torment.
It is not the end of existence.

But truth rarely alters denial in the minds of men and women.

Denial Doesn't Change Reality

Billy Graham has this to say about why he believes people tend to deny hell:

> Certainly war, hunger, terrorism, greed, and hatred are hell on earth, but, except for the Bible believer, a future hell became part of the ash heap of ancient history. As hell was becoming for many no more than a swear word, sin was also an accepted way of life. People began to look to science, education, and social and moral programs as possible solutions to the growing chaos of an insane world. If people can ignore what the Bible calls sin, then they can quite logically discount what it says about the reality of hell.[42]

We refuse to spoil the present over concern for the future. But then when the future becomes the present, we're always sorry we didn't exercise our foresight.

Prepare for your future. Planning for retirement in your later years is wise, but paying little attention to the inevitability of your encounter with timelessness is foolish indeed. A lifetime is but a few short years. Eternity is forever. Don't let it be the ants-and-the-grasshopper story all over again. The ants prepared for winter while the grasshopper fiddled. Don't be a grasshopper. Don't fiddle around with hell.

With so much at stake, playing ostrich and sticking your head in the sands of denial doesn't seem very bright to me. Ignoring reality doesn't change it. The odds on the Bible being wrong are too remote. No document has been more scrutinized over a longer period of time and stood the test any better. Its truth defies the odds makers. But we shouldn't be surprised. After all, God wrote it.

The odds of the Bible being wrong are long indeed. Not believing it is a bit like mortgaging your home to buy lottery tick-

ets. The odds stink big time. It's the same with hell. You're playing some long odds if you don't believe that place is to be avoided
at all costs.

It is not my intent to do an exhaustive study on hell. I just
want to let you know that nice people go there, and to give you
some idea of what's in store for those who do go. With that in
mind, here are a few glimpses of that awful place called hell. Its
descriptions are enough to make your skin crawl.

Glimpses of Hell

Some people think hell is going to be like being on the sun.
The gravitational pull would make it hard to move around, and
it's so large they'd probably never come into contact with anybody else. If they did, it would be two people with their sin
nature, turned totally loose, so they'd be at each other's throats
the whole time. They could never leave because of the gravity
and they'd have the torment of the heat of the sun, and yet somehow wouldn't be consumed.

I doubt if the sun illustration is possible because the Bible
says hell will be outer darkness. But it could be literal fire.
Consider your basic Bunsen burner. The tip of the blue flame
inside is the hottest part of the flame. The outside of the flame is
relatively cool. But the coolest part is at the base of the flame
where the combustible material becomes gaseous and ignites. It's
a place devoid of light. We can see it only because of reflected
light. What's the definition of darkness? The absence of light.
Hell can be literal flame and be a place of utter, outer darkness.

Have you ever been in an underground cave? So deep that
there was no light at all? The guide warns you and then turns out
his light. You wait for your eyes to get used to inky blackness, but
nothing happens. There is no adjustment to be made. There is no
light. Part of hell will be absolute darkness for eternity, coupled
with a conscious awareness of the pain produced by fire. Absolute
aloneness, total darkness, and unending agony. Only the screams

of the others also suffering in hell.

Here's an unknown writer's opinion of hell:

> There's no way to describe hell. Nothing on earth can compare with it. No living person has any real idea of it. No mad man in wildest flights of insanity ever beheld its horror. No man in delirium ever pictured a place so utterly terrible as this. No nightmare racing across some fevered mind ever produced a terror to match even the mildest hell. No murder scene with splashed blood and oozing wound ever suggested a revulsion that could touch the borderlands of hell. Let the most gifted writer exhaust his skill in describing this roaring cavern of unending flame and he would not even brush in fancy the nearest edge of hell.

The commentators I read collectively agree; hell will be a place where there will be no righteousness, it will be a dimension that's absolutely and eternally separated from God, and it will be an abode of constant judgment and retribution. The word "hell" carries with it the connotation of doom, hopelessness and futility.

Hell is both a place and a condition. One writer phrased it this way:

> Life apart from God is existence filled with guilt, hollowness, despair, meaninglessness, and helplessness. The agony of eternal punishment apparently involves both body and soul because Scripture says both are ultimately cast into hell. Apparently this would involve inner anguish as well as detrimental effects upon the body. It may involve the torment of being cut off from fellowship with one's fellow man, and also the results of living within a society of men from which the grace of God has been completely withdrawn.[43]

Chafer says of hell, "No more decisive terms could be employed than those which describe men as being *without Christ, without promise, without God*, and *without hope*."[44] But you ought to know that no one is in hell right now. The dead who don't know Christ aren't there yet. They're in Sheol-Hades.

Sheol-Hades

In the Old Testament there is a place called Sheol. In the New Testament it's called Hades. It's the same place, the words are basically synonyms. Some writers call it Sheol-Hades.

During Old Testament times, everybody who died, both the righteous and the unrighteous, went to Hades. But there were two levels, the penthouse and the basement.[45] The penthouse was like heaven and was a nice place to go. The basement was like hell, not as bad perhaps, but it was a terrible place to be.

The righteous Old Testament saints, such as Abraham, who believed God and were counted as righteous, went to the penthouse. The unrighteous went to the basement. One commentator wrote, "It appears from this passage (Luke 16:19–31) that Hades is composed of three compartments: 'Abraham's bosom,' 'the great gulf fixed,' and 'the place of torment.'"[46] The heaven-like place is called Abraham's bosom and is separated from the place of torment by a chasm.

Christ died, and during his three-day period in the grave went to both Hades and paradise. He went to Hades and took all those in the penthouse to a place of paradise called heaven, the place Christ had prepared for them, the place where God lives.

Tim LaHaye agrees with this scenario:

> We know that the Lord Jesus went to paradise, for in Luke 23:43 he told the thief on the Cross who cried out for salvation, 'Today you will be with Me in Paradise.' So we know that Jesus went directly from the Cross into the paradise section of Sheol-Hades. Now look at Ephesians 4:8–10. This passage reveals

that paradise is no longer located in Hades, but was taken by Christ up into heaven. This would indicate that the believer now goes to heaven, where he is joined with the Old and New Testament departed saints, leaving the former paradise section of Hades an empty compartment.[47]

Since that time, those who die knowing Christ (who are spiritually alive) don't go to Hades. They go to heaven. Jesus left those who were in the basement. They will end up in hell—but not for awhile. Several events have to unfold before that happens. I'll talk more about that in a minute.

By the way, currently nobody has a body in either heaven or hell. Everyone exists in spirit form only. But those in heaven get their new bodies before those who are in the basement do.

Spiritual Bodies

Both those in heaven and Hades are there in an intermediate, bodiless, spirit state. This state is both conscious and immediate upon death.

As I studied this material I began asking why the ancient patriarchs didn't go straight to heaven. I liked this answer best:

You are probably wondering why the Old Testament saints were directed to the place of comfort or paradise in the first place. After all, they believed in God while they lived. The answer is found in the inadequacy of the covering of their sins. In the Old Testament, sins were temporarily covered by the blood of a 'lamb without blemish or without spot.' But an animal's blood was not sufficient to permanently cleanse their sins (Hebrews 9:9–10). Sacrifice was an exercise of obedience, showing their faith that God would someday provide permanent cleansing from sin through the sacrifice of his Son.

When our Lord cried from the Cross, 'It is finished,' he meant that the final sacrifice for man's sin was paid. God in human flesh could accomplish what no animal sacrifice could ever do—atone for the sins of the whole world. After releasing his soul, Jesus descended into Hades and led all the Old Testament believers, held captive until sin was finally atoned for, up into heaven, where they are presently with him.[48]

Since the time Jesus emptied the penthouse, all people who are spiritually dead when they physically die go to Hades, the basement . . . that's all that's left. The penthouse has been moved to heaven. But as I said, we only go as "soulish" or spirit. We don't have bodies in either place. Not yet, anyhow.

Then, when history ends, at the end of the age, a series of final events will take place. Some seem a bit bizarre, but it's bizarre that Christ is looking forward to spending eternity with you and me in the first place. So, don't get hung up in the unusual nature of things. Remember, what seems strange to us doesn't matter at all if the whole deal is real. Our ways are not God's ways. If it is real, you can't pick and choose on this deal. Folks can argue about some of the little things that aren't clear, but the significant events in the Bible are too well documented to legitimately dispute. Those in the know generally agree on the following end-times events happening (although they do argue about the sequence):

1. The rapture (the taking of Christians out of this world when the dead in Christ get their spiritual bodies).

2. The tribulation (three and a half years of good times on earth without any thought of God, and three and a half years that will be absolutely the worst in the history of the world).

3. Armageddon (the last final battle at the end of the tribulation).

4. The coming of Christ (ending the battle that would have destroyed the populations of the earth).

5. The Millennium (a thousand years of peace on earth under the reign of Christ). The beast and the false prophet (who are satan's henchmen during the tribulation) are the first to be thrown into hell (the lake of fire) at the beginning of the period. Satan is bound and sent to a pit for a thousand years with his demons.

6. At the end of the Millennium, satan will be turned loose for a short time to test the faith of those born during the thousand year period.

7. The Great White Throne Judgment (the spirits of the dead in Hades will be united with their respective eternal, new bodies and will be judged along with those alive at the end of the millennium).

8. The casting of the unrighteous into hell. Satan is first (remember, the beast and the prophet are already there), then his demon followers, and then the unrighteous.

Items 1 and 7 in the above list mention getting new bodies. Those in heaven will get a new body similar to the one Jesus had after the resurrection. He walked through walls, enjoyed eating, was touched, flitted around between heaven, the upper levels of Hades, and earth, and had a body like Peter, James and John saw at the transfiguration:

> There he was transfigured before them. His face
> shone like the sun, and his clothes became as white
> as the light. (Matthew 17:2)

Whatever kind of body Jesus had at that event is the kind of body we'll get at the time of rapture. The new bodies of those who physically died spiritually alive in Christ will be united with their spirit first. Then those Christians who are alive at the time of the rapture will get their new bodies as well. We'll talk more about that in the next chapter.

Those in Hades will get their new bodies at the time of final judgment at the Great White Throne. The Bible describes it as follows:

> The sea gave up the dead that were in it, and death and Hades gave up the dead that were in them, and each person was judged according to what he had done. (Revelation 20:13)

Dead bodies are scattered about the earth and the sea in various states of decomposition and dissolution. The God who made 'em in the first place is the same God who will put 'em back together in a "changed" state. The word death in the above passage means the grave. In other words, all the dead bodies of the lost will unite with their respective spirits from Hades. But they will have a different kind of body than when they were physically alive. This body is the hell-bound counterpart of an anatomy like Christ's resurrected bod'. This new body will experience and withstand the torment of hell, and it will join together with its spirit, which will endure eternal punishment as well. It's a kinda double whammy retribution reunion, lasting forever. We're talkin' "bad berries" for the live-ins . . . but it will be even worse for the devil.

What About Ol' Sloughfoot?

Satan, who was locked in a pit for a thousand years at the beginning of the millennium, will be loosed for a short season to flush out those who were born during that time who hated being under Christ's authority. Then the devil will be cast into a lake of fire, hell—the destination God created for him in the first place.

As previously mentioned, satan will be preceded into this final fire by his two tribulation-period henchmen. When Jesus Christ returns, both the beast and the false prophet, those evil ones used by the devil himself, will be thrown into hell at the beginning of the millennium. They appear to be the first to go in. Satan will follow a thousand years later.

There appear to be levels of punishment in hell. The Bible suggests punishment according to works on this earth. But this conclusion may come from our failure to see the casual sinner being as bad as Adolf Hitler or Saddam Hussein. I don't have God's perspective. The result is that I see a scaled difference between sins. Standing up close, I see a one-to-ten scale. From a great distance, perhaps from God's viewpoint, the scale looks like a single dot. At any rate, if there are levels in hell, the deepest part of the pit is being reserved for the devil himself. The beast, the false prophet and the demonic host (the angels who sided with satan at the time of the fall) will apparently be at another level. People will then be positioned according to their works at the upper levels of hell. The concept of degrees of punishment is consistent with the parallel concept of rewards in heaven, so it's a likely scenario.

I was speaking to a group of junior highers at Hume Lake Christian Camp in California a few years ago. We were outside around the fire circle and I was doing my heaven and hell talk. I told about the levels of hell, how satan would go in first and deepest, and how the demons would go in next. It was then that some kid in the back row yelled out, "And then the Celtics!"

Being a former LA Laker, and having been beaten by the Boston Celtics in the seventh game of the NBA national championships by one basket, the thought made me smile for a moment. We even burst out laughing. But I wouldn't wish hell on them, although some of them will end up there, along with a bunch of the Lakers and the rest of the players in the league who don't decide to follow Jesus Christ.

By the way, don't make the mistake of thinking satan is going to rule in hell. He won't be sitting on a throne holding his scepter laughing at the plight of others. Hell was created for his torment. All those who agree with his philosophy will join him, but hell wasn't created for them; it was created for the devil. But he'll not rule there. Satan will be in torment and all those with him will be in torment as well.

One thing is certain. Mick Jagger made a bad deal and Cindy Lauper was wrong. Cindy said she could hardly wait to go to hell, because that's where all her friends would be, and they would be able to party forever. Wise up, Cindy, there will be no party in the lake of fire. The screams you'll hear will not be "party hardy" sounds.

A Good Look at a Bad Place

In Luke 16 we get a glimpse of what Hades is actually like. We can make some assumptions about hell from our observations. I call it the story of the rich man and Larry.

> There was a rich man who was dressed in pur-
> ple and fine linen and lived in luxury every day. At
> his gate was laid a beggar named Lazarus, covered
> with sores and longing to eat what fell from the rich
> man's table. Even the dogs came and licked his sores.
> (Luke 16:19–21)

There was a rich kid who dressed well. "Clean!" "Slick!" Very together. GQ, look out! Whatever is "hot" right now wherever you live is what he had plenty of. He also lived it up daily. In other words, he was a total "party animal." They called him Sweet William the Third.

Bill had it all. Electrostatic rock monitor speakers with a bass booster were in the corners of his room. The best CD and DAT recorder, along with all the finest audio equipment, were in their places against the wall. The biggest, highest-resolution tube TV with Surround Sound was centered on the opposite wall. He got all the satellites, of course. And a well-stocked refrigerator was next to his bed. Our "moneyed man-about-town" drove a new Corvette with a super "amped" sound system. Of course he was great looking and was one of those unusual teenagers who didn't have any zits. Our affluent athlete was a standout jock; the star quarterback on the football team, high scorer on the basket-ball team, the top track guy, and hit .600 for the baseball team.

The luscious lover was great in the girl department, got straight A's without studying, and was student body president as well. What can I say, the guy was a "stallion," "Sir Studly," a "Mister Everything" for sure.

The son of the gardener was named Larry (Lazarus just doesn't make it). He lived by the entry to the estate in the gate-keeper's cottage down below the rich kid's house. Larry had a pretty tough life. He had some terrible zits and was covered with sores. We're not just talking simple pimples here. Larry had Acne Vulgarus. His was a severe case.

To make matters worse, Larry had to eat the rich kid's garbage. And to top it off, the poor guy didn't get paid enough to afford a doctor. The medical plan for Larry was obviously defi-cient, because instead of a prescription for his face or some "Oxy 10", they got a dog to lick his zits. (See verse 21, "even the dogs were coming and licking his sores.") How gross! Poor Larry. (Remember, I didn't write this stuff. You'll have to take this one up with God.)

> The time came when the beggar died and the angels carried him to Abraham's side. The rich man also died and was buried. In hell, where he was in tor-ment, he looked up and saw Abraham far away, with Lazarus by his side. So he called to him, 'Father Abraham, have pity on me and send Lazarus to dip the tip of his finger in water and cool my tongue, because I am in agony in this fire.' (Luke 16:22–24)

It came about that this poor, pitiful, and pathetic person died and went to heaven. I think the doctor diagnosed Larry's cause of death as a case of infected zits.

The very next day Sweet William was driving his "Vette," wrapped it around a tree, was killed, and went to Hades. Looking up, the rich kid saw Larry in the penthouse.

The first thing we learn about Hades, and probably about

hell, is that the rich kid knows what's going on in the penthouse.

> Those who go to hell will probably know what they
> missed out on in heaven . . . forever.

As to how that happens in utter darkness I don't have a clue. We know from other Scriptures that those in heaven won't know what's going on in hell, because there will be no sadness or sorrow there. But if Hades is like hell, it looks as if the residents will always be aware of the cost of dying spiritually dead. They will always be aware of what they missed.

The second observation comes when the rich kid hollers out a demand to the penthouse, "Send Larry down here to comfort me."

Can you believe it? He's still trying to boss Larry around. This pompous, once-opulent juvenile still has his personality intact, but all the good parts have been removed. Only the negative elements remained.

Can you imagine spending forever with a bunch of people who have their unrestrained sin natures turned completely loose? Me neither. Or even worse, how about enduring eternity completely alone and isolated with only your absolute rottenness to contemplate? Yuck!

Then our "money bags moppet" says, "Have Larry touch my tongue with a drop of water; for I'm in agony in this flame." Notice—he is suffering. Pain and anguish are characteristics of hell. There is flame, and he is in the middle of it.

> But Abraham replied, 'Son, remember that in
> your lifetime you received your good things, while
> Lazarus received bad things, but now he is comforted
> here and you are in agony. And besides all this,
> between us and you a great chasm has been fixed, so

that those who want to go from here to you cannot,
nor can anyone cross over from there to us.' (Luke
16:25–26)

The fourth point of the passage is the great chasm that
exists between heaven and hell.

> Once you're there you are there forever.

The gap can never be crossed. Never! Either way.

This passage of Scripture eliminates the possibility of any
kind of purgatory. You can't run a few of your laps in hell and get
out for the rest. There is no serving penance and cutting out for
the promised land. No sir! The canyon can't be crossed.

> He answered, 'Then I beg you, father, send
> Lazarus to my father's house, for I have five brothers.
> Let him warn them, so that they will not also come to
> this place of torment.'
> Abraham replied, 'They have Moses and the
> Prophets; let them listen to them.'
> 'No, father Abraham,' he said, 'but if someone
> from the dead goes to them, they will repent.'
> He said to him, 'If they do not listen to Moses
> and the Prophets, they will not be convinced even if
> someone rises from the dead.' (Luke 16:27–31)

When Sweet William understood the eternal nature of his
fate, he begged the guardian of heaven to tell his five brothers
about the reality of hell so they wouldn't have to go there.

The gatekeeper reminded him, "We've told them already,
we gave them the Bible. They wouldn't read it."

The kid said, "No, do something spectacular, like bringing
somebody back from the dead. Then my brothers will believe."

"We did that too," the gatekeeper responded. "We did it with Jesus. You didn't believe him. They haven't, either. Like you, your brothers will have no excuse."

The rich kid was burning. There was no escape. He had made his decision while physically alive, but found no opportunity to change it in eternity. "He had sunk to a death beyond prayer, a condemnation beyond forgiveness, and a doom beyond the reach of Christ."[49]

Assuming Hades is hell-like, the story of the rich man and Larry gives us a few peeks into what hell will probably be like. To get a more complete picture, I looked up the verses about hell and reduced them to words and phrases so as to put the biblical characteristics in concise form. The list follows:

1. You'll keep your personality with your sin nature turned loose.

2. Satisfaction is never available, there is never any fulfillment.

3. An absence of all that's good.

4. In the presence of all that's bad and evil.

5. Unrestrained demonstration of selfish urges.

6. Continual burning.

7. Consuming fire.

8. Unquenchable fire.

9. Eternal destruction.

10. Outer darkness.

11. Weeping and gnashing of teeth.

12. No presence of God.

13. No glory of God's power.

14. Lake of fire.

15. Burns with brimstone and fire.

16. Second death.

17. Extreme anguish.

18. Worse than death itself.

19. Degrees of punishment.

20. Wrath and fury.

21. Tribulation.

22. Distress.

23. Sudden destruction.

24. No escape.

25. Pits of nether gloom.

26. Torment goes on forever and ever.

27. They have no rest.

28. They know what's going on in heaven
    and are aware of what they missed forever.

That's a thumbnail impression of hell. Pretty grim, huh? Interestingly enough, some people think life on this earth is more important than their existence afterward. Hell is a terrible price to pay for such distorted values.

Stay out of hell. You don't want to go there. It's the pits—literally. The other option is much better. Heaven! All those who die in Christ (spiritually alive at the time of physical death) will go there. We'll take a look at the place Jesus called paradise in the next chapter.

CHAPTER SEVEN

HEAVEN
(Upside potential.)

Three people have seen heaven—Jesus Christ, John in Revelation, and Paul. Jesus made it. John saw it in a vision. Paul probably went there and came back. We're going to study Paul's account of heaven just like we studied the rich man's account in Hades.

Paul saw heaven after he'd been stoned. (That's the New Testament version of the word stoned, not the current interpretation. It referred to rocks, not drugs or booze.)

There were three kinds of stoning in Paul's day. The first was a legal or judicial method. Officials built a scaffold, eight to ten feet high. Accusers would throw the accused off and try to drop a rock on his chest or head. Then everybody would stand around in a circle and throw rocks.

The second manner of rock throwing was called "pit stoning." It was the primary method of enforcing capital punishment. The pit was eight to ten feet deep and fifteen to twenty feet across. Accusers would throw the accused in and everybody would encircle the hole and throw rocks until "the dude" was dead.

The third way was a plain old "lynch mob" kind of stoning. The mob would make a circle around the accused and chuck rocks at him until he was dead. People didn't like this method very much because if someone sidearmed a rock, and really hucked it hard, but missed, somebody on the other side of the circle would end up getting hit.

You can understand why the folks preferred the pit stoning method as the capital punishment of choice. It was safer for everyone—except the accused. And it was cheaper than having to build a scaffold. Paul preferred it, too. He held everyone's coat while Stephen was stoned. There was a time when he loved seeing those Christians get "rocked." But what goes around, comes around. The apostle probably didn't notice who was grasping the garments when he got his. He was in the pits. The story comes from Acts 14:8–20.

Paul, Barnabas, Titus and company had been chased out of Antioch and Iconium, so they hiked the twenty or so miles to Lystra. Taking a lesson from Jesus and Peter, they found the most noticeable crippled man they could find. When you heal one of those guys they have a tendency to leap up and run and jump and praise God all over the place. It never fails to draw a crowd. So that's what Paul did, and sure enough, the "healed hobbler" drew a crowd.

But Paul hadn't "boned up" on his local history and wasn't prepared for what happened. Tradition had it that the Greek gods Zeus and Hermes had come to town generations earlier and apparently only one family had shown them the proper courtesy. So the "gods" snuffed all the townspeople except the household who showed them a good time. It left such an impression that the folks who resettled Lystra built a church and actually staffed it with a priest, just in case the gods ever returned.

So when Paul and Barnabas did their thing with the lame guy the people thought Zeus and Hermes had come back. Not wanting to mess up twice in a row they tried to worship the traveling band of miracle workers. It was a natural mistake. Barnabas was tall and statuesque, like Zeus. And Paul certainly had a special command of the language, just like Hermes, the god of orato-ry. Archeology has confirmed the existence of the temple dedi-cated to the gods, and a plaque commemorating their return shows a date that corresponds with the time the apostles would have been there.[50] We don't know who the original "gods" were (probably a couple of demons or demon-possessed guys like the beast and the prophet from the last chapter), but the whole deal is real. Archeology has confirmed it.

As Paul and Barnabas were negotiating with the townsfolk as to where they ought to direct their worship, trouble makers from Antioch and Iconium arrived. The folks at Lystra changed their tune in a hurry. Peer pressure oftentimes does that.

How quickly they forget. How fleeting is glory. Heroes one minute, targets the next. The same thing happened to Jesus and it's about to happen to Paul. As a future warning, it will happen to anyone who takes a stand for Christ, you included. They'll love you one minute, but they'll hate you the next. That's the way it is for those who follow him. There will be persecution for the believer.

Paul's stoning probably went something like this: (This is pure conjecture on my part, something straight out of First Carty and Second Hesitations, but it will make the account more inter-esting.) The mob moves in on Paul. The others undoubtedly get roughed up in the process, but the mob centers their attention on Paul because he's the talker.

The people probably beat Paul for a while and then threw him into the pit. Falling on the rocks strewn in the bottom of the pit from previous stonings, Paul gets cut up a bit and bruised badly. People surround the rim and begin throwing. The apostle scrambles to his feet.

Paul is holding his hands up to protect his head. He doesn't see the two-hander coming at him. The boulder strikes him on the lower part of his leg, shattering it, crushing his foot, causing the apostle to fall to his knees.

That's when another big, heavy, two-hander comes at him. Paul tries to dodge, but he can't move. The rock catches him in the chest, dislocates his shoulder, breaks his clavicle, and knocks the wind out of him. The blow drives him to the ground.

Now he's on his side gasping for air, lying on the only hand he can move. The other is useless. He has no protection for his head. And here comes another big one. There is nothing he can do so he watches it all the way in. The rock hits him in the eye and crushes the side of his skull. They kept throwing rocks until the body was just barely visible, but Paul didn't know it. He was probably dead. But that's not the end of the story.

Afterward, the delegated officials climbed into the pit, pulled Paul out from under the rocks, pronounced him dead, hoisted him out of the pit, dragged him out of town, and left him for the dogs to eat. That's the way it was done in those days.

Victims of pit stonings were either dead or not far from it. Those who survived were hardly capable of travel. Weeks or months of rest and rehabilitation would be required to put a person back on his feet.

But the Bible says that while his disciples stood around him, Paul got up, walked back into the city, checked things out, and the next day started a sixty-mile trip with Barnabas to Derbe. In other words, God worked a miracle and healed Paul while his followers watched.

It must have been like a fast-forward scene in a movie. The wolf man losing his fangs and hair and becoming human as we watch the screen. Cinderella at the stroke of midnight returning to what she was before her fairy godmother waved the wand. The flower closing in the evening in a time-lapse nature film. As the disciples watched, the cuts healed, the broken bones mended, and the bruises went from red, to blue, to yellow, to healed. It was a miracle. And God fixed it all—well, almost all.

Fourteen years later, Paul wrote about what happened next. He saw heaven:

I know a man in Christ who fourteen years ago—whether in the body I do not know, or out of the body I do not know, God knows—such a man was caught up to the third heaven. And I know how such a man—whether in the body or apart from the body I do not know, God knows—was caught up into Paradise, and heard inexpressible words, which a man is not permitted to speak. And because of the surpassing greatness of the revelations, for this reason, to keep me from exalting myself, there was given me a thorn in the flesh, a messenger of Satan to buffet me—to keep me from exalting myself! (2 Corinthians 12:2–4,7)

He's not sure if he died or not. He probably did, but he's not sure. Paul says, "I know a man in Christ (me) who fourteen years ago, whether in the body or out of the body (Man, I don't know if I was alive or dead!), God knows. Such a man (me) was caught up in the third heaven." (Jesus referred to the sky above as the first heaven, the planets, stars, and the universe beyond as the second heaven, and the place beyond, where God dwells, as the third). Paul went on and ends up saying that he was caught up into paradise (heaven) and heard and saw some things that were so fantastic that he was forbidden to tell anybody about them. And just to remind him not to tell, God gave him a thorn in the flesh.

Here's a wild guess as to what that thorn was. We know Paul had some kind of an eye problem. It's possible that God healed everything except where the rock smacked him in the head. And the reason he didn't heal the eye is because what Paul saw was so incredible that when he came back, if he were able to articulate all he had seen, people would want to commit suicide so they could get to heaven faster than planned, thereby circumventing the process God had intended for them on this earth.

Regardless of how it came about (and I doubt it happened

the way I've told the story), I'm convinced God left Paul with a thorn in the flesh to remind him not to tell all that he saw, for our benefit. Heaven is that wonderful.

> God gave us enough information to cause us to look forward to heaven, but not enough to cause us to forget those around us who aren't going.

Although there are two-thirds more verses on hell than there are on heaven, God still has much to say about paradise. There are five hundred and fifty references to it. Here are a few more glimpses.

Heaven

During the four hundred years of silence between the writing of the last book of the Old Testament and the first book of the New Testament, some of the words for God and heaven actually became synonyms. The New Testament word for heaven often means God. Sinning against heaven means sinning against God. In some instances the Kingdom of Heaven means the same as the Kingdom of God. The Bible tells us heaven is filled with God, so being in heaven will put us in the actual presence of God forever. Heaven is continually being with God. It goes beyond the perfection of the Garden of Eden in that we'll be with God all the time. Not just when he comes to visit. We'll always be visiting 'cause we'll live there. What an incredible thought.

In addition to God being there, everything that ought to be important to us is there, including our Savior, name, inheritance, reward, treasure and citizenship. Fellow believers from both Old and New Testament times will be there. And the angels of God are there as well.

The Bible calls heaven a place, and God's Word says that it is up. Paul was caught up, Jesus ascended and descended, and numerous verses refer to heaven as up.

> If no matter where you stand on earth heaven is up,
> then the third heaven must surround the second
> heaven.

Scientists are concluding that the universe is spherical. Therefore, the expanse that exists beyond wherever the heavens end (planets, stars, galaxies, etc.) is where heaven begins (where God lives). John MacArthur says, "Heaven encircles our universe and is as big as our God."[51] That makes him very big indeed. But it does make heaven a long way away. Or does it?

How many light years is it to heaven? Who knows? We haven't figured out how big the universe is yet. But Jesus said to the thief on the cross next to him, "Today you will be in paradise." They would make the journey in a hurry. Today! They must have a heavenly warp drive. No! Faster than that. More like "Beam me up Scotty," one of the great phrases from "Star Trek." The transporter in the Enterprise took a person's molecules apart in one place and reassembled them in another. It sounds as if we'll have a heavenly transporter of some kind, doesn't it?

Because Christians are predestined to be conformed to the image of God's Son, we will have bodies like the one Jesus had. Just like Jesus did with the thief, he will enable us to flit around heaven and the heavens at will.

What kind of body did Jesus have? He ate but didn't have to. It looks like he did it because he liked to eat. Chowing down is a satisfying experience. So he ate.

In Oregon, local strawberries are only available for a few weeks. We have to import our strawberries from Texas, California and Mexico at other times of the year. I love strawberries, but we can't afford the out-of-state berries. Besides, the local berries are better. So Mary always buys two big boxes of local berries when they are ripe, and I try to eat them before they spoil. In other words, I try to O.D. on strawberries to get a fix that will last me the rest of the year. I love the challenge, and I love strawberries. But let's face it, I love to eat.

Traveling around the country speaking makes for lots of eating out. When I'm invited to a home for dinner, folks always do their specialty. It's not unusual for me to gain five pounds from Saturday to Wednesday. I have to work out pretty hard between trips to maintain my weight.

Imagine eating whatever, whenever, just for the taste of it—but it won't have to be "lite" ice cream and Diet Coke! What a fun idea. I'm looking forward to heaven. Not just for the food of course, but won't that be a fun part? Imagine, doing your shopping on the planets of the universe and eating the produce of the galaxies. Sounds great to me.

In addition to eating, Jesus appeared suddenly, walked through walls, could be touched, flew, talked, and was transfigured (his body was brilliant like the sun). His body was also perfect. No physical impairments. No aches or pains. No parts wearing out. No sore lower back, no stiff neck. And we'll get one just like it.

We weren't designed to be disembodied spirits. We are terrestrial creatures. We need a bod, so God made us soul and body. Those of us who die in Christ prior to the rapture will be separated from our body until that time of reunion. Then God will put the bodies of the saved dead back together in a glorified form and unite them with their respective spirit. When I come together with my new bod', if I have a choice, after thanking God, I'm going to eat some strawberries. Fun! And then I'm going to dunk a basketball, from the waist. I've always wanted to do that.

The Bible tells us there will be a new heaven and a new earth. And the capital city of the new heaven will be a new Jerusalem. This is not a book on heaven so I'll leave that detail for your further study. Just be aware that we'll need bodies so we can walk around town when we don't want to fly. A resurrected body is part of the experience of heaven. Wow! What a deal.

Heavenly Summary

But wait, there's more.

It's kinda like a television commercial. If you buy the "widget," you'll get a "chingadeer" at no extra cost. And if you order right now, they will throw in a "whatchamacallit." There's a whole lot more to heaven than flying around in a new body, eating everything in sight.

John MacArthur described heaven on one of his tapes as follows:

> Heaven will be perfect freedom from all evil forever. Never a sinful thought. Never a selfish thought. Never an evil word. Never a useless word. Never an evil deed. Never defiled. Never unclean. Never imperfect. Always doing everything which is perfect and holy. No doubts, no fear of God's displeasure. No temptation. No persecution. No abuse. No division. No discord. No disharmony. No disunity. No hate. No cruelty. No fights. No disagreements. No disappointments. No anger. No effort. No prayer (there will be nothing to pray for). No fasting (there will be nothing to fast for). No repentance (there will be nothing to repent of). No confession (there won't be any sin). No weeping (there will be nothing to make you sad). No watchfulness (there will be no danger). No trials. No teaching, no preaching, no learning (we'll have all spiritual understanding and there will be nothing to learn). No evangelism or witnessing. Perfect pleasure. Perfect knowledge. Perfect comfort. We will love as Jesus loved, absolutely and perfectly. And we will have perfect, complete, unending joy.
>
> In heaven we'll never have to apologize, we'll never have to confess, we'll never feel bad. We'll never have to make any corrections, never have to

clarify, never have to explain what we really meant, and we'll never have to straighten anything out from confusion because nothing will ever be confused. We won't have to fix anything, repair anything, adjust anything, or replace anything because nothing will ever wear out or malfunction. Never have to help anybody, nobody will need help. Won't have to deal with satan, demons, or sinners. Won't have to defend ourselves, there will be no attack. We'll never cry, never be alone, never be lonely, never be hurt emotionally or physically. We will never have to be cured, counseled, coddled or entertained. We'll always be filled with joy. Never have to do anything special for anybody because everything we do will be special to everyone all the time. There will never be any grief. We'll never lose anything, never miss anyone, and we won't have to be careful because we won't ever make a mistake. We won't have to plan for contingencies or emergencies, because there will never be a Plan B. We'll never have to avoid danger because there will be no danger.

Heaven is the experience of eternal perfection of body and soul.[52]

But wait! There is still more. I did the same thing with the verses on heaven as I did with the verses on hell. The following is a summary of what God wants us to know about where he lives:

---

1. The place where God dwells.

2. A place of righteousness.

3. We can worship God there. (By the way, if you don't like to do that now you might find you won't have the opportunity to do so later.)

4. No hunger.

---

5. No thirst.

6. No tears

7. No death.

8. No sadness.

9. No pain.

10. No hard labor.

11. Always be with the Lord.

12. Paradise.

13. Beautiful.

14. Magnificent.

15. Nothing unclean.

16. God will be our light.

17. Lots of places to dwell. (It took God six days to make this world, Christ has been working on heaven for almost two thousand years. It should be nice.)

18. No sex. (I have a friend who said, "Man, if there's no sex in heaven I don't want to go." My physical relationship with my wife is fantastic, but if everything in heaven is better than that, let's go. Heaven must be great.)

19. New and perfect bodies.

20. Every spiritual blessing is ours.

21. Physical descriptions of heaven use all the things that are the ultimate in beauty to us (gold, silver, crystal, precious jewels).

22. Retain our present personality, with sin nature (flesh) removed.

---

23. No age. (Somehow every person will be distinctive, just as they are now, except they will not appear young or old.)

24. We'll be served by the angels.

25. We'll be served by Christ.

26. Not limited by time.

27. In charge of many things.

28. In heaven we're going to worship, reign, and serve proportionate to what we have done here on this earth with the time, talent and treasure we've been given.

29. In heaven we'll do all the good things we do here only we'll do them perfectly. The things that we enjoy here we'll have the opportunity to do there in a perfect state.

Go back and contrast the characteristics of hell with those of heaven. There's quite a difference, isn't there?

It's Inconceivable

Where would you like to spend forever?

That sounds like a dumb question, doesn't it? Who in his right mind would choose hell over heaven? Yet the Bible tells us that most will make that very choice. I'm reminded of the buzz word from the movie Princess Bride— inconceivable. But I know why. Most do not believe that nice people really do go to hell. The majority of people do not believe the whole deal to be real.

Is it real? Consider this, "Every shred of evidence for the resurrection of Christ is evidence for eternal life in heaven."[53] If Jesus Christ conquered death, then there is a heaven. All that Easter stands for is proof of heaven. And the Holy Spirit is a pledge, a payment of earnest money. Consider him an engagement ring, the promise of the glories of heaven to come. What great thoughts! But it won't mean much if all we do is think about it. We need to live in the light of heaven.

Looking toward heaven is an evidence of salvation because we have a heart that is set on God and we want to commune with him. We should be making life's decisions with our eyes on heaven. And we need to make sure our friends understand what they run the risk of missing.

I don't know where you are spiritually as you read. I don't know if you are an on-fire, goin'-for-it, no-holds-barred, Jesus-lovin' believer; if you are lukewarm; or if you are new to the things of God. If you're on fire, perhaps this book will encourage your passion for those who run the risk of missing heaven. If you are lukewarm, my prayer is that these words will be energized by the power of God to fire you up. If you are new or confused, let me pose a question.

The Diagnostic Question

Here's a diagnostic question. If you were what we call dead and were standing before the gates of heaven as a voice boomed out saying, "By what right do you desire to enter my heaven?" What would you say?

Perhaps your response would be, "Uhhhhhhh, I was a good person. I was born in the United States and I never murdered anybody."

"A good person?" the voice might say. "Compared to whom?"

Timidly, you might respond after stammering and stuttering, "Hitler."

"Yes, you compare well to Hitler, but how do you compare to Christ? He is the standard. You must either be as good as Jesus or have his recommendation to get into this place. I know you aren't as good as he is, so will he stand up for you? Have you stood up for him? Do you know him? Are you a friend of my son?"

Actually you won't have a thing to say. Romans 3:19–20 says you'll be silent in your sins. You'll know that an all-knowing God is totally aware of your sin and that there will be no "snowing" him. You can't "shine" God and you'll realize it.

At a time like that you won't need a lawyer. You'll have already been pronounced guilty. What you'll need is someone to pay your fine. . . . There is good news. Someone did.

Jesus asked Peter, "Who do you say that I am?" Peter had the right answer. "You are the Christ," he said. "My Savior" is what he meant. "I'll accept your payment on my behalf because I can't do it on my own," is the heart of his response.

Jesus is asking you the same question right now. But the fact that you stink may keep you from hearing. Your odor will definitely impact your decision making.

Now don't be offended. We all stink. It's because we are onions. We'll talk about that next.

CHAPTER EIGHT

WHO GOES WHERE & WHY?
(The Golden Rule.)

God always operates by the "Golden Rule." (He who has the gold makes the rules.) God's got all the gold and he definitely makes the rules. Either play this game called life his way, or try to be your own god and go to hell. That's one of his rules.

Some of his rules may seem a little strange sometimes, but don't forget who is perfect and who isn't. Having to trust someone else with our eternal destiny seems bizarre. That's what we have to do when we rely on Christ to resolve our sin. (Remember, it's our sin problem that causes us a hell problem.)

Why can't we resolve the issue of heaven or hell on our own?

How good would a person have to be to get into heaven without help? Perfect! Because that's what God is, and heaven is where he is. And there will be no imperfection in heaven. It's part of the Golden Rule.

Are you perfect? No, you're an onion. You stink. Sin does that to a person.

We're All Onions
The next time you're with friends, sniff 'em. Really! Just give them a big sniff. Check out their scents.

Let me tell you what you'll smell. You will either smell their stink—or you will smell something covering up their stink. Why? Because we all stink. It is our nature. Sin creates stench. We have all done it, therefore we all reek. You got your dad's stink, and you gave yours to your kids. Face it. You're an onion.

What happens when you put an onion in the refrigerator? It stinks up everything inside. That's why you can't go to heaven as an onion. If you could you would stink up high heaven.

Imagine yourself on the family room floor and someone opens the refrigerator door. What comes wafting across the room with the cold air from the 'fridge? Stink! The onions have done it again. But how badly they stink depends on the kind of onion.

Bermuda onions are just about the worst. Eat a big slice on a burger just before bed time. Talk about morning mouth! Your dog will especially love you.

Walla Walla onions don't stink like other onions. They're the best. So are Maui onions. People argue over which have the least odor.

Leeks, chives and green onions are somewhere in between.

We measure stink by comparing onions to onions. But that's the wrong standard. We think Walla Wallas and Mauis are the best because they stink the least. But any onion will still ruin the food in a refrigerator, including the two least stinky. The standard is not which onions stink the least.

> God's standard is the absence of stink of any kind.

God is holy and pure. It doesn't stink where he is. So nobody who does, even just a little bit, is going there.

Man was created in God's image, but that doesn't make God an onion. We didn't become onions until Adam and Eve uttered the first "no" to him. Sin and death were the result, and that was the origin of our sin nature. Adam was made in the image of God. We were born in the image of Adam—with a sin nature. From that point on we were disqualified from heaven on the basis of our own merit. Why? Because as onions we would make heaven stink.

Let me summarize.

1. We stink.

2. Stink isn't possible in heaven.

That creates a serious problem. What can be done? I'm an onion and I wanna' go to heaven. The first option is cooking. Cooking an onion will get rid of some of its stink.

The first chance you get, sniff an old person. Just walk up and sniff 'em. You'll notice that he doesn't smell as bad as a younger individual. Why? Because life has cooked some of the stink out of 'em. But cooking doesn't solve an onion's total odor problem just as living life won't prepare you for heaven. A cooked onion will still stink up a refrigerator.

Since cooking won't solve the entire problem of an onion's stink, ultimately God is faced with one of two decisions. (1) Dispose of it. Throw it in the trash or grind it up in the disposal—hell. That's what I am trying to warn you against. Don't let it happen to you, or to the nice people you know.

Or, (2) wrap it in Saran Wrap—cling wrap, Handi Wrap, or "zip lock" that sucker. That will do it. Then you can put it in the refrigerator and it won't stink up the place.

When we place our faith in Christ we are new creatures in him—new creations, spiritual birth has taken place—we are born again. So to make the "wrapping" concept correct, we have to imagine an onion wrapped in Saran Wrap. Then unwrap it. When the onion layers are peeled off, what would you expect to find? Nothing, because an onion is nothing more than stinky layers. But something happens when you wrap up in the Handi Wrap of Christ. A miracle occurs. An onion doesn't have a core.

So a seed is planted in the center and a piece of fruit begins to grow. As it grows, as you conform to the image of his Son, the onion layers get thinner and thinner. After a while there are only a few stinky layers wrapped around the outside of the fruit. Some scholars call the layers that remain "flesh"—old worldly habit patterns left over from living in this world. Others call the layers the remain of our sin nature. Whatever, it's the last of Adam's influence on you.

Regardless of what it's called, the source of the stink that remains is what the Apostle Paul struggled with in Romans 7:15–25. A paraphrase goes something like this, "I wish I hadn't done what I just did. Why did I do it? I didn't want to. But I did it anyway. I don't want to do it again, but I probably will. Why do I do the things I don't want to do. There is something in me that fights with what I ought to do." Paul had just described the remaining layers of onion wrapped around the fruit that had been created when spiritual birth occurred.

Even though there is a little onion left on those of us who know Christ, just remember, God has X-ray vision. When he looks he sees a piece of fruit—the new creature in Christ. It's the fruit that goes to heaven to await its joining with a new body. And that new spiritual body has had the last its layers peeled off.

Onions don't go to heaven. But you were born an onion. However, you can't get into heaven unless you are a piece of fruit, or unless you are perfect (with no smell). Since you already smell, the second option is not possible. You really only have one choice. Wrap up in Christ and let him create some fruit, or go to hell.

Perhaps an understanding of perfection will further illustrate this point.

Are You Perfect?

Watterson's *Calvin and Hobbes* is one of my favorite comics. Just prior to Christmas[54] Calvin is on the front of his sled, his "come-to-life" stuffed tiger Hobbes is on the back and they are having a discussion.

Calvin begins, "I'm getting nervous about Christmas."

Hobbes answers with a question, "You're worried you haven't been good?

"That's just the question. It's all relative. What's Santa's definition? How good do you have to be to qualify as good?"

Calvin has just asked a "big time" question. He continues as they zoom between trees on their way down the hill, "I haven't killed anybody. See, that's good, right? I haven't committed any felonies. I didn't start any wars. I don't practice cannibalism. Wouldn't you say that's pretty good? Wouldn't you say I should get lots of presents?"

Hobbes offers a deep thought and probes with his reply, "But maybe good is more than the absence of bad."

It's a thought Calvin has considered. "See, that's what worries me."

Calvin doesn't know how good "good" really is. But he wants to tip the scales in his favor. So he asks Hobbes, "Okay, assuming I can get an overnight letter to the North Pole, what would you charge to write me a glowing character reference?"

Hobbes knows Calvin's heart. You can tell by his response, "Oh no, I'm not going to perjure myself for you! My record's clean."

Neither one of them is sure what good is, but both are pretty sure Calvin is not whatever it is. However, Hobbes thinks his record is clean and is therefore okay. He considers himself to be good. Both have concluded that being good is a relative term.

Everything is relative to a standard. Time is measured by a single clock kept in Greenwich, England, and all other clocks around the world are set in accordance with the one that is considered to be the standard. Your timepiece is only accurate when it is set exactly with the one that serves as the gauge for measurement. The Bureau of Weights and Measures keeps the standards by which all the other weights and volumes around our country are measured. Your scale is only accurate when it weighs exactly the same as the standard kept at the bureau.

We cannot afford the technology necessary to keep our measurement devices in tune with the standards at the bureau. Temperature, moisture, pressure, corrosion, and all the other factors altering a perfect environment are too difficult and expensive for us to maintain. So we settle for something that is within acceptable limits. In other words, something less than the standard. Concepts such as "good," "better," "best," "nice," and "good enough" are the result. Comparisons are being made to a standard when such words are used. But none of these ideas have any meaning apart from the standard that defines them.

Something other than the standard is only perfect when it is in every way equivalent to the standard. God is perfect. So is Jesus Christ. Both serve as representations of the same standard of perfection.

God's standard is Christ. All comparisons are made to him. But we tend to think that "nice" is good enough because we make our comparisons to each other.

With time, weights, and measures we determine what is close enough for the need. Thus the word "tolerances." Building a house requires less precision than building a shuttle craft. You need a more accurate thermometer to measure the heat generated in a high-performance racing engine than in an oven baking a turkey. We settle for less than perfection, because perfection is either not possible, not necessary or too expensive to achieve. But God doesn't acknowledge tolerances in heaven. It's part of his Golden Rule. "Close enough" is a term we devised (or was it government workers?). Let me explain what I'm trying to say using baseball as an analogy.

Through onions, measurements, baseball, and basketball, I

have tried to show you how we make comparisons to each other, rather than to the standard of God, when determining the relative concept of "good enough." I hope you understand what I'm trying to say by now, but you still may be dealing with the issue of the fairness of it all. If the Golden rule is a problem, perhaps three definitions, along with a few conceptual illustrations, will help clear things up a bit.

Justice (Getting What We Deserve)

Justice has been defined as getting what we deserve, mercy as not getting all we deserve, and grace as getting something we don't deserve at all. Let's start with justice and try to understand why we don't want it.

As I was proofreading this portion of the manuscript, I happened to be flying from New York to Denver. The in-flight movie was "Defending Your Life." The plot caught my attention. It was timely, so I added the following "review."

It seems the star is killed in a car wreck and wakes up in Judgment City. There are a defender and a prosecutor assigned to his case, along with two judges to rule on whether he has to go back to earth in another life, or press on as a citizen of the universe, to begin learning to use more and more of his brain. But you can't become a citizen until you're able to conquer your fears. Selected portions of his past were reviewed on video tape and then debated.

While in Judgment City, he meets a woman who is a good person and who has her fears under control. They fall in love, and during their last night together she invites him to sleep with her. He decides not to for several reasons, including being fearful of what it might do to them wherever they end up going next.

According to the movie, the "right thing" was to make love to this woman, but instead, he is condemned for doing the right thing, which was refusing. So the result of their evaluation was: she would be "moved on," but he wouldn't pass because he still had fear.

It's not surprising that neither heaven nor hell exists in the universe that is portrayed (denial prevails). Nor should I expect morality to be considered a virtue (this is a Hollywood production). The only criteria for "moving on" is being a "good" person and overcoming your fears. God has nothing to do with anything.

In the movie, if you hadn't sufficiently gotten over your fears, you got justice (which was going back to earth as many times as it took to get it right.) That "New-Age" treatment is a long way from a biblical scenario and has a snowball's chance in you know where of being true.

People who don't understand the God of the Bible somehow convince themselves that his attribute of love will overcome the mandate of his holiness—which is the absolute necessity of carrying out justice. (This is something very different than what was portrayed on the screen.) Judgment City in the Bible is the Great White Throne, where there is no trial or debate. There will be no "going back until you get it right."

> Justice demands an irreversible hell.

As a result of that understanding, unlike in the movie, I don't want you to overcome your fear. As a matter of fact, my preference is that you be overcome by it. Be afraid for yourself if you don't know Christ. You should. Be terrified for your friends who don't know him. It will be a natural outcome if you understand the truth.

Assume I am the star player on a high school basketball team and I'm out with a really cute girl. Curfew is at 10 P.M. It is now 9:40. I have a decision to make.

The penalty for breaking curfew is a chewing out by the coach and running twenty laps. I want to kiss this girl goodnight, but I need more time. She's not ready to "lay a lippy" on me yet.

The chewing out is no big deal, and having run twenty laps

at other times in my basketball career, I know what that feels like. I can handle it. But I have never kissed this girl before; I don't know what that feels like. And if I take her home now, I don't think she'll kiss me. I need a little more time.

I ponder for a few moments, "What to do, what to do?" "Twenty laps is tough . . . but the girl is really cute." Naturally I decide to "go for it" and to take whatever I have coming to me at tomorrow's workout.

The next day at basketball practice, the coach says, "Carty, judging by the smile on your face you broke curfew last night. Is that true?"

"Yes sir," I reply with a grin of satisfaction.

"Well, don't stand there talking. Start runnin', we'll talk later."

Consider these questions:

Who made the rules?

Sure, the coach, of course.

Who chose to break the rules?

That's right. I did.

Did the coach decide I would run twenty laps, or did I?

I made the decision, the coach just enforced the rule.

Some people say, "How can a loving God send so many people to hell?"

Consider these questions as a response:

Who made the rules of life?

God did.

Who breaks his rules?

We do.

Who decides who goes to hell?

We do! God just enforces the rules. In other words, we do the sending.

Lewis Sperry Chafer said, "the marvel of it all is not that sinners are lost, but that they are ever saved."[55] In other words, we shouldn't be surprised that nice people really do go to hell.

Justice is getting what we deserve. And nice people deserve justice as much as anybody else does. Baseball and onions prove that.

Understand one thing clearly. God does not want you to go to hell. His desire is to spend eternity with you. "The Lord is not slow in keeping his promise, as some understand slowness. he is patient with you, not wanting anyone to perish, but everyone to come to repentance." (2 Peter 3:9) When you think about it, it's hard to believe that God wants to spend eternity with any of us. I know what I sometimes am in my private times. I know what I am deep down inside, and I don't like it much. Some of the stuff that comes out of my nature is disgusting. And you know what you are. Some of your thoughts are terrible, too. What's scary is that we are capable of such awfulness. We're onions. And yet, God wants to spend eternity with me. You too. God loves us anyhow, buthe will let us have our own way. If it's separation we want, it's separation we'll get. Left to our own devices, we'll get what we deserve . . . justice. And justice means hell.

Do yourself a favor. Don't ever get pious and pray for justice.

The last thing in the world you want from God is
what you have coming to you.

Think about it. What if God gives you what you deserve? I don't want him to be just to me. I want my past forgotten. Judge me on the basis of some other criterion, because judgment based on my past means hellfire for sure. No, sir, when it comes to sin I don't want to get what I deserve. I'm an onion and I stink!

There you are, probably sitting comfortably as you read. Although you deserve justice, nothing has happened to you . . . yet. Time continues to pass, and nothing is happening. So if you don't know Christ, unless you die in the next few moments, what you are experiencing is mercy.

Mercy is a little extra time for you to appropriate grace—so you don't have to endure justice. Keep reading while I explain.

Mercy (Not Getting All You Deserve)

There I am, the basketball player who broke curfew, running my laps. As I finish my tenth trip around the floor, the coach looks over and yells, "Carty, how many laps have you run?"

Panting, I holler, "Ten."

Then he says, "Sit down Jay, rest a while and I'll see if I can find someone else to run the other ten for you."

I should have had to run twenty all at once, but the coach let me rest after ten. What a guy! That's mercy . . . not getting all I deserved.

Do understand, this illustration does not apply to hell. It's impossible to run ten laps in hell and get out for the other ten. The Bible makes it clear, once you're there, you're there.

But the story does apply in this way. I'll bet you are well fed. (Probably better than you ought to be.) And you are most likely living in a decent apartment or house. (Nicer than most people in the world.) And you are well clothed. (At least by the world's standards.) In other words, things aren't too bad for you right now. Sure, your situation could be better. There are a few hassles going on in your life. But compared to most people in the world, things could also be much worse for you. Isn't that right?

If, as you are reading this, you do not have a personal relationship with Jesus Christ, I have good news for you.

> Unless you die in the next few moments,
> God has given you a little more time . . .
> some more time to find Christ.

In other words, you're not getting all you deserve. You deserve justice, but he's giving you more time to respond to Christ. That's called mercy. But grace is something totally different.

Grace (Getting Something We Don't Deserve)

Our basketball player shows up the next day after breaking curfew and the coach asks him about staying out late. The player tells all.

Here's the problem. The rule is fixed. Not to enforce the rule makes the coach a liar, which he is not. Everybody knows that. Twenty laps have to be run. That is the penalty.

To the surprise of the player, and the whole team as well, the coach says, "Sit down son, I'll run your laps for you."

I've played basketball for lots of coaches over the years. And I can tell you for sure, not once has a coach ever even thought about running my laps for me, let alone done it. Yet that is exactly what Jesus Christ did for us. While we were still onions, Christ ran our laps (Romans 5:8).

God gives you two choices (remember, the extra time you get to make the decision is called mercy): (1) pay the price for your sins (justice), or (2) accept the payment that was made on your behalf (grace). A song says, "He paid a debt he did not owe; I owed a debt I could not pay." Jesus paid our debt so we wouldn't have to. What was our part in the deal? Nothing, we're onions.

We were both the "reason" and the "beneficiaries" of the death of our Lord. But God thinks we are worth saving, even though we caused the debt he paid. Wow! We don't deserve it, but he did it anyhow. And in spite of what we are, Jesus Christ is looking forward to spending eternity with each person who chooses to follow him. He wants to serve you.

We will worship him, but he will serve us. He washed the disciple's feet as an example of servant leadership. The same will be true in heaven. Christ will actually serve us in heaven. I cried when I realized it. Wow! That's a great big double WOW!!! That's grace.

Keep this in mind. Grace is offered to all people, the good as well as the bad. It's available to folks who seem to be better than some and to those who aren't perceived as being good enough by others. Christ died for nice people and for those who aren't so nice. And he did it because God can't love in degrees. He can only love perfectly. That means he loves us all the same, regardless of what we've done. So he died for all people in all walks of life who will accept what he did, regardless of the comparisons we make with each other.

What about nice people who don't accept Christ's payment on their behalf? You guess'ter Chester. Unless they're perfect, they go to hell. Being nice has nothing to do with anything eternal.

There are some very nice people in this world who are trying to make "it" on their own. Others are trying to get "there" using the philosophies and religions dreamed up by men, women, and movies. But there is only one "school of thought" that God cooked up. And nice people who decide not to do life God's way will spend eternity separated from him. Why? Because they haven't repented.

> Repentance is agreeing that I can't stand before God
> and be okay on my own merit.

Repent! Ya' gotta! It's part of the Golden Rule.

I'm running out of room to write and reasons with which to

beat you over the head. You've had enough time to check form and consider the odds. It's time to place your bet. Eternity's your choice.

CHAPTER NINE

THE LAST BUTTON ON JEB'S SHIRT

(It's time to choose.)

I was to speak at a men's retreat and I had entered the camp dining room for dinner. I joined four guys at their table, in the only seat available. Without an introduction, having recognized me as the speaker, even before I could take a bite, the man across from me said, "I have cancer."

That was it. No other words. No lead-in, no preparation, no nothin'. As it turned out, he was telling the truth. He did have cancer. His approach was certainly abrupt, and I didn't know if he was trying to shock me, or if he really wanted a response. I think my reply would have been the same regardless of his motive.

Not being the compassionate counselor type, I looked him in the eye and asked, "Are you ready to die?"

He wasn't. He didn't know Christ. Bet he came to know him before the weekend ended.

Are you ready to die? You're not if you're lost.

Can you imagine being lost and not knowing it? It's possible. Let me tell you about my friend Maurice Russell.

Maurice, his son Jeff, and Jeff's dog Uggi went backpacking in the White Mountains of Arizona a few years ago.

The goal was to spend a weekend drawing closer to his fifteen-year-old son.

They weren't experienced but they had some equipment, including a tent, sleeping bags, a compass, a map, and three days of food. Figuring a canteen of water to get them from the trail head to Tonto Creek, they started out eagerly on a sunny Friday morning. It took four hours longer to find water than was planned. After a good drink, a little fishing, and a romp in the creek, the day was over. They enjoyed their first night under the stars and looked forward to two days of hiking up Tonto creek to Bear Flat.

The hike on Saturday and Sunday was more difficult than either had expected. Actually it was quite treacherous. The danger made it much slower going than either of them had prepared for. Jeff had a date on Sunday night and keeping it was real important to him. If they made Bear Flat by noon on Sunday, everything would be fine.

Saturday was a great, but trying, day. They finished it with trout and popcorn. Things were going well. But on Sunday, noon came and went and Bear Flat hadn't come into view. Jeff blamed the whole thing on his dad, and as irritation mixed with disappointment, strong words started flying. So much for bonding. Then it started to rain. Bear Flat was not to be found.

By evening everything was wet, including their sleeping bags, and the food was gone. They had to settle for the uncooked trout they caught. It was too wet to get a fire started.

Jeff had missed saying good-bye to the girl who was going back to her home in the Midwest. He spent the night hot with anger as he shivered in a wet sleeping bag.

The dog was as tired of trout as Maurice and Jeff were, and the walk wasn't fun anymore. Cuts, blisters, scrapes, and irritation filled their thoughts. More words about poor planning and dumb ideas filled the air. They continued to hike, thinking that Bear Flat was around the next bend in the creek—it never was.

The compass looked as if the rain had ruined it. It showed them going northeast, yet they knew they were going north. And north was where they would find Bear Flat. Besides, they had to stay with the creek. At least it provided liquid and food, and they knew it flowed into the Flat. They didn't bother with the compass anymore; it was unreliable. And they knew Maurice's wife Nancy would be worried. She didn't know they were fine. It was just further to Bear Flats than they thought and the trip required more time than they had set aside.

On Tuesday, being over twenty-four hours overdue, they saw a plane in the sky that they thought might be looking for them. Jeff had spotted a helicopter on the horizon too. So they spread out a white sheet and flashed a signaling mirror. They were too tired and hungry to travel right away anyhow.

Forty-five minutes later, as they were breaking camp, a "Hello" came from behind them. It was a National Guardsman. The helicopter had dropped him off while the chopper went back for fuel. After a half-hour hike to a clearing, the helicopter appeared. Five minutes later they were at the coordination headquarters where a crew had been directing more than fifty people in the search.

Never once had either Maurice or Jeff thought of being lost. They just assumed they hadn't arrived yet. But a wrong turn had been taken and they had been walking up Hegler Creek, not Tonto Creek. It was a common mistake. The rescuers knew right where to find them. Father and son had been lost . . . but neither had known it.

There are a lot of nice people out there who have taken the wrong turn in life and are walking up the wrong canyon toward what they think is Bear Flat. "If I lead a good life I'll be just fine," is the conclusion of most. "Nice people don't really go to hell." They are lost and don't know it.

People choose to believe their own reasoning over trust-worthy sources. It happens all the time. Trusting our instincts over a compass as to which way is north isn't uncommon. Neither is trusting the philosophies of men over the directions of God. Why do people continue to rely on themselves and treat the Bible like it's all wet? Because they are lost and don't know it.

Yes, it's possible to be lost and not know it. That was Maurice's problem. It might have been yours, but not any more. I've been careful to tell you the whole story. Nice people really do go to hell. You may be lost, but at least you know it.

It is one thing to be lost and not know it, but it's quite another to be lost, know it, and not acknowledge it.

My backpacking buddy Don Snow directs the Rocky Mountain High program for Officers Christian Fellowship out of Spring Canyon in Colorado. They conduct Christ-centered outback experiences for military personnel. He told me a great story that fits right here.

One drizzly evening in July, a pack train had brought a barbecued chicken dinner surprise to the participants. At high altitudes hypothermia is always a concern, so a soft rain is never to be taken lightly. And dehydration is always an ever present threat. A person has to drink a surprising amount of water to stay hydrated. These are just two of many mountain killers. Getting struck by lightening, falling into crevasses, and getting real lost are other good ways to die.

As dinner was cooking, a family in wet shorts and tee shirts came walking by. Everyone was shivering and thirsty. The dad was macho. Mom and the two teenage boys were miserable and let it show. They had climbed Mt. Yale that day but they had come down the wrong canyon and had been lost for more than five hours. They hadn't had food or water since morning.

"Where's a trail?" were the first words out of the man's mouth. It embarrassed him to have to ask.

Noticing he had said "a trail," not "the trail" Don replied, "We'll have some food in about ten minutes and a hot drink in about five. Looks like you folks could use some refreshment."

The woman and the boys were nodding and looked relieved until the dad shattered their hopes. "Nah, we don't need nothin'. Just tell me where a trail is."

"Well, it's about fifty meters right through the woods."

"When I get to the trail which way do I go?"

"Where's your car?

"It's at Denny Creek trail head."

"You go down.

"When I get down and I get to the road what do I do?"

Don told him to turn and go back up the hill. The man was so lost he didn't even know if he should go up or down when he got to the main road.

As soon as they left Don told his people, "That was a really good example of how folks die in the woods. They were lost and confused, cold and hungry, but he wouldn't say, 'Yeah, we could use some help.' He wouldn't even let the members of his family eat or drink."

Harold, the wrangler who had brought the food for the barbecue, is a fun cowboy. He was reflecting on the comin's and goin's of the family. "My truck was down there," he said. "I could have had them drive it to their car. It's gonna' be plum dark before they get where they're a-goin'."

We reflected as to why the man wouldn't accept the help he needed. Our conclusion? Pride! He put himself and the members of his family in jeopardy because of his pride. Mr. Macho didn't want his family to receive help because he refused to admit it was his lostness that had gotten them in trouble.

My friend Don tried to be like Christ to that vain, shivering father. He offered food and drink to meet the family's immediate need. He was ready to guide them down the canyon to make sure they were safe. And Harold had a truck for them to drive to where they were parked. Everything the family needed was available to them. But the dad was too proud.

Are you a parent who is lost? Which way are you leading your children? Acknowledge your lostness and change directions—for their sake as well as yours!

Are you a teenager who has been going the wrong way? Are your friends going too? Confess it. Change destinations.

There's a strong word that describes those who are too proud to receive help when they need it. The man in the mountains filled all the criteria . . . fool. So does anyone who denies the probabilities of hell. It's so hard to convince some people. The odds on the Bible being wrong are so remote. But facts don't mean much to a fool. I guess that's why the Bible has so much to say about them.

"The way of a fool seems right to him, but a wise man listens to advice." (Proverbs 12:15) I've said it before. Let me say it again. The sixty-six books of the Bible, written by forty authors, over sixteen hundred years, in several countries, in three languages, being in perfect harmony with each other and all other factual historical, archaeological, and scientific works, both current and past, is a miracle of God's preservation that can't be denied. Only a fool would fail to heed its advice.

"The discerning heart seeks knowledge, but the mouth of a fool feeds on folly." (Proverbs 15:14) To deny the reality of hell when the Bible speaks about it more than any other topic is foolish indeed.

"A fool finds no pleasure in understanding but delights in airing his own opinions." (Proverbs 18:2) God has made himself crystal clear. Of what use is man's opinion when it contradicts God? Only a fool would listen to a fool, and only a fool would speak against the Father.

"As a dog returns to its vomit, so a fool repeats his folly."(Proverbs 26:11) Some people never learn. Only a fool continues to stand in opposition to God.

I was exposed to fools some years ago when I was at UCLA working toward a doctorate in the field of public health. I have often thought back to a research project in which I was involved.

A test group was given a series of driver reaction tests. The time it took each person to move his right foot from the gas pedal to the brake pedal in response to a visual stimulus was measured. Then the subjects each consumed two beers and sat for ten minutes. Afterward, the reaction test was administered again. Although alcohol levels were well below the definition of legal intoxication, the reaction times of every test subject were significantly slower.

That part of the study was not surprising. But in each instance, those being tested felt their reaction times after drinking the two beers were better than before. They were all surprised by the findings. Further, it was very difficult to convince them that the data was correct because it so completely went against what they thought was true. Several even chose to reject the findings in favor of their own perceptions, and still feel the same way today.

The study reminds me of the old saying, "I've made up my mind. Don't confuse me with the facts." It's the response of a fool.

Dear friend, consider this carefully. If the Bible is God's Word, then it must contain the facts. It has clearly established itself to be God's revelation to us and it emphatically says that nice people really do go to hell. You may not think those statements are true, and you may be sincere in your belief. But which is more likely to be correct—you or the Bible? "Me!" is the response of a fool.

Are you one of those who have had a couple of beers? You think you're just fine, don't you? Your mixed-up perception of God has given you an inflated opinion of yourself. *How could a loving God send somebody like me to hell?* Is that your thought? *There will be a whole lot of genuinely bad people going before I do.* Is that your conclusion? You're right. There will be a lot of people in hell . . . BEFORE YOU GET THERE!

The Last Button on Jeb's Shirt

My dad has some great old Missouri sayings. One of them is, "We're down to the last button on Jeb's shirt." It means we're almost through.

I've said it as many ways as I can. I've driven my editor nuts by using more illustrations than I'm supposed to. I've been redundant beyond words. I've broken all the rules of writing. But I'd rather mess up by saying it too many times in too many ways than fail to say it enough. Now we really are down to the last button on Jeb's shirt.

If you believe nice people go to hell and take ownership of the problem by recognizing yourself as the onion you are, there is still one more step—take a close look at the Son of God. Have an encounter with him and see what happens. Few who have encountered Jesus Christ have come away unchanged. Your heart will either be softened or hardened. Ask him into your life and he will come in. If you do you'll never be the same. Actually, you won't be the same even if you don't—but you won't be saved from your sin.

You'll Never Be the Same

Pilate couldn't wash his hands enough. Although he didn't become a Christian, his meeting with Jesus Christ had permanently changed him. After trying four times to release Jesus, he followed through on ordering His death. But Pilate would never be the same. Christ had left His mark on the man.

So it was with the soldier at the foot of the Cross. "Surely this man must be the Son of God," he said or prayed. We're not sure which. Either way, he was a changed man. If he prayed, the Roman was also a saved man. If he only gave intellectual assent, he was still lost in his sin.

My favorite encounter of all was with the cohort of soldiers marching into the Garden of Gethsemane before daylight, the morning Judas betrayed Jesus.

A cohort was at least fifty men. On one occasion it was six hundred. But usually a cohort represented three hundred soldiers. Therefore, we can assume three hundred macho guards were marching through the city that morning before daylight to arrest one man.

Little hob-nailed sandals. You could hear 'em all over town stirring up dust in the stillness of that hour. Townspeople were probably getting up and following.

Little leather mini-skirts. Little red tassels on their heads. What a sight!

"Halt, one two!" was the shout of the captain as he approached the man Judas had kissed. "Are you the guy they call Jesus?" was His demand of the Son of God.

"I am he," is what your Bible says Jesus said. But that's a poor translation. What Christ really said was, "I AM!" Don't mistake that for "I am." "I am" would be a statement of acknowledgment. "I AM" is something else indeed. That's the name that came out of the burning bush that talked to Moses.

It was the name of Yahweh, the unspeakable name of God. A Jew would never say it. Lips were too unclean. Jesus had in essence just screamed, "I'm God, and you're lookin' at him!"

The power of Jesus speaking that name made bowling pins out of the cohort. Three hundred macho soldiers were knocked on their macho behinds. Neither Josephus, nor any other contemporary historian ever refuted the occurrence. My friend, it is historical fact.

I can see one of those big, burly men standing up, dusting off his rear end, and asking, "Hey, what was that?"

His buddy pointed toward Jesus and replied, "I don't know, but it came out of His mouth."

And with a huge smile I can imagine Jesus saying, "Okay, you can take me now. I just wanted you to know who you were messin' with."

Do you think the soldiers would ever forget that day? I doubt it. They might not have entered into a personal relationship with Jesus, but they would never be the same.

That's the way it was in those days when you encountered Jesus. That's the way it is today, too. Few there are who encounter him who walk away unchanged.

You may not receive Jesus Christ, but you will never be the same.

Your heart will either be softer or it will be harder. But it will not remain the same.

It's Time to Take Temptation Captive

It is time for your encounter with Jesus.

Are you ready?

Stop reading for a moment and think about your answer to the following question.

Who do you say that he is?

You're close aren't you?

I guarantee that satan won't let you get away easily. What you think about next may determine where you'll spend eternity.

You must take your thoughts captive to the obedience of Christ.[74] Don't allow yourself to think about that tempting thought. Satan doesn't want you to consider Jesus.

I know how the devil works. Your mind is wandering right now. You're having trouble concentrating. The phone's been ringing or someone has come to the door. There have been interruptions and distractions. You're having trouble thinking. Isn't that right?

Stop!

Consider what's happening. You're in a spiritual battle. And it's over your soul. At least acknowledge that.

Fence Sitters Are Uncomfortable

I have a passion for your soul. I haven't been awakened in the night in a cold sweat about it, but I do value your soul sufficiently to stay up late writing and to endure the process of editing so that you might read these words. I have spent many an hour thinking through this book and praying for the concepts that might be used to push you over the fence. Here comes the last nudge.

If you are on the devil's side and want to stay there, there isn't much that can be done for you. But if you are straddling the fence, you are probably uncomfortable. That hurts like crazy, especially if you're a guy. I'd love to push you over to the Lord's side.

Why don't you give up? You may never be closer to accepting what Jesus Christ did for you than right now. Why don't you pick up the phone and give God a call?

Pick Up the Phone

This is how the whole deal works.

As I said, my daughter is a missionary in Africa. Pause for a moment and holler, "Hello, Kim."

Yell as loudly as you can. Put a little something extra into it. Go for it. "Hello Kim."

Did she hear you? No. She is too far away.

What's the best way to talk to her? Sure, the telephone.

Do you want to talk to God? Understand that "Oh my God!" won't cut it. That's an expression of a worldly exclamation. If you want to talk to God you have to know his Son.

If the whole deal is real, to talk to God you have to pick up Christ (the phone), and then his Holy Spirit (the wires or microwaves, or satellites, or whatever) does the work to make God's phone ring in heaven. Apart from Christ, prayers are nothing more than talking to the floor or the wall. They don't go anywhere. The only ones he answers, if you don't know Jesus, are the ones that will lead you to him. And that's the one I want you to pray right now.

It's Time to Act

I have a Macintosh portable computer that I use to write when I'm on the road. Scrapbook is a software program that provides a place where text and pictures can be stored for future use. I rarely use it. However, as I was working on this chapter, gathering the verses on the fool, there was a piece of text waiting there in Scrapbook. I do not know the source. I don't remember ever reading it. I certainly don't recall putting into my computer. So, the author is unknown, but the words are perfect as you are confronted with asking Jesus Christ into your life:

"Remember this as you consider your answer.
Man has made himself/herself the center of every-

thing in this world. But God will be at the center of everything in heaven. The decision you made or will make, either for or against Christ, should be measurable by what your life revolves around. If it's not God, you won't like heaven. And you probably won't get to go there."

Do you want to stay on the throne of your life, or do you want Jesus Christ to be there?

Consider 1 Chronicles 28:9 before you respond:

". . . for the Lord searches every heart and understands every motive behind the thoughts. *If you seek him, he will be found by you; but if you forsake him, he will reject you forever.*"

Those are your options. Seek him or be forsaken. Put him in authority of you life or face his judgment. Turn to God, don't trust yourself. Receive what Christ did. Make your choice

This prayer will help you:

Dear Lord,

You are an awesome God and you know that I don't fully understand everything that's happening right now. This whole thing is too new to me. But I'm responding to what I believe is right. Father, I'm a sinner and I want to turn from my sin to you. I realize now that Jesus Christ did die for my sin and I want to claim what he did for me.

Jesus, I receive what you did; I want forgiveness, and I want you to have full control of my life. Thank you for coming into my life as you promised and thank you for saving me from hell. I commit myself to a journey of both learning about and serving you.

Does this prayer express where you are? Can you pray it with your heart, as well as your voice? Do you want God in control of every aspect of your life? Then, by the promise of God's Word, the problem of sin and separation from God has been resolved in your life.

Hooray!!!! You made the right choice.

Congratulations.

How Do You Feel?

Some people cry. Some people realize how lost they were and weep tears of joy, gratitude, and relief. Some people get very excited, hear bells, gongs and buzzers, get goose bumps, and whoop and holler over the awareness of their new, intimate relationship with God.

But most don't feel much different at all. Perhaps just an inner peace or cleansing knowing that all is finally well with their soul.

So don't depend on feelings for the assurance of your salvation. If you do, you'll always be wondering, "Am I or am I not?" The Bible says that if you confessed with your mouth, and believed with your heart, you are all set :

> That if you confess with your mouth, 'Jesus is Lord,' and believe in your heart that God raised him from the dead, you will be saved. For it is with your heart that you believe and are justified, and it is with your mouth that you confess and are saved. (Romans 10:9–10).

Sin Will Still Be a Problem

Even though you're saved from the consequences of your sin, you still have some old sinful patterns to break. So you'll still blow it now and then (Read Romans 7:15–8:2 again and remember that the Apostle Paul struggled too).[56]

Your new goal is to let Christ in you lengthen your times between stumbling, and when you do stumble, to shorten the time it takes you to confess it with a repentant heart (1 John 1:9).[57]

Of course the best goal is not to sin at all. Remember, temptation is not a sin. So that first thought or feeling isn't sin, but dwelling on it is. So claim 1 Corinthians 10:13:

> No temptation has seized you except what is common to man. And God is faithful; he will not let you be tempted beyond what you can bear. But when you are tempted, he will also provide a way out so that you can stand up under it. You don't have to sin.

If You Received Christ

Congratulations! Way to go! You just made the most important decision of your life.

Welcome to the family of God. I'll have the pleasure of meeting you some day and you can tell me all about yourself. Fun, huh?

If you received what Christ did for you, it becomes important to tell a fellow believer, and to begin spending some time learning more about what you've done. Therefore, call the person who gave you this book or the church or bookstore where you got it and tell somebody what's happened. Then find a good church where the Bible is taught and start attending regularly. You need to start the process of being discipled. So you'll need a good study Bible. You'll find one in a Christian bookstore.

If You Have Not Received Christ

My prayer is that God will not lessen the pull on you nor will he give up on you, but instead will grant you more time.

However, if you are still not moved, please remember:

> For the Lord searches every heart and understands every motive behind the thoughts. If you seek him, he will be found by you; but if you forsake him, he will reject you forever. (1 Chronicles 28:9)

There shouldn't be any doubt about the purpose of this book by now. Let me summarize. I'm bettin':

God is real.
 The Bible is real.
  Jesus Christ is real.
  Hell is real.
   Heaven is real.
    The whole deal is real.
     You're gonna' die.
      There is nothing more valuable than a soul.
      Nice people really do go to hell.
       You have to bet on the whole deal.
       Eternity's your choice.

Did concepts collide?

Do you believe that the whole deal is real?

Did you bet on Jesus?

Hope so!

That's it. We're through. Finished!

Live long and prosper . . . in the Lord.

THE SAFEST CHOICE
(Pascal's point.)

I had just sat down for another plane ride from somewhere to somewhere else. Places and planes tend to run together when you travel a lot. I've got a million and a half miles logged with United Airlines alone. It was a cattle car flight. Every seat was full.

I like an exit row window. There is a bit more room for my 6' 8" frame and I have someplace to prop a pillow for sleeping. I carry an inflatable pillow for my back, I snag two pillows for my head and a blanket to keep my arm and leg warm as the inside of the plane tends to radiate the cold from the outside. But there would be no snoozing on this flight. Not this day. The Lord had other plans.

Sometimes you just want to be alone. It's easy to get "peopled out" in the ministry. That's why I carry ear plugs. You never know when you'll get a screaming kid close by. This time I didn't get a chance to put them in. The guy next to me wanted to talk.

He was a clean cut businessman. Well dressed. Boyish in appearance, but in his early forties. He was an auditor for a large freight company. *Kinda' looks like a "bean counter,"* I thought.

"What do you do?" he asked.

"I'm a traveling speaker," was my reply. I've learned not to say the word "evangelist." The stigma is too great.

"What do you speak about?"

"Values and morality."

"Where and to what audience?" He was persistent. It was time to come clean.

"Mostly in churches, but I speak at retreats and for special meetings sometimes. I'm a travelin' preacher, I use the Bible as my text and I talk about Jesus Christ." I knew what was coming next.

"For what denomination?"

"I'm an inter-denominational kinda guy. I cross denominations with what I have to say, so it's hard to pin me down. I speak in all kinds of churches."

"Have you ever spoken in a Mormon Church?"

"No," I replied. "I've never been asked."

We chatted about family and kids and politics and we were in total agreement with all of that. Then he asked me a blockbuster question after making a very kind statement.

"I am comfortable talking to you and I'd like to learn. Help me to understand something. Most Protestants don't believe Mormons are Christian. Without trying to convert me will you tell me what you think?"

I had read a bit about Mormonism and have listened to a couple of tapes over the years, but never have I discussed it in this way. I started with Christ. "It all revolves around Jesus Christ and who he really was . . . and is."

"I agree totally," Tom (not his real name) said as he jumped in. "Christ is everything. I love him so much. So what's the problem?"

"Tom there are Christians who are culturally Christian, some who are Christian by association and those who are Christian because of a personal relationship with Christ. Western culture tends to identify with Christianity, but that doesn't make a westerner Christian. Neither does being raised in a Christian home. I know some Baptists who are Baptists because their parents are Baptists, but who don't have a personal relationship with Christ. The same can be said for Catholics and for Mormons. And since my daddy was a bookie I tend to think of things in terms of odds. So of the three, if I had to bet, I'd bet that proportionally there would be more Baptists who had a personal relationship with Jesus Christ than Catholics, because Catholics tend to believe taking the sacraments, belonging to the organized church and doing good works will save them from their sins more than Christ will. Any time you water down the person of Christ your odds of being saved are diminished greatly. Would you agree?"

"Yes," he exclaimed enthusiastically.

"But I'd bet that the proportion of Mormons who are saved is even less yet."

"Why?"

"Because you have a watered-down Jesus."

"What do you mean?"

"I believe the Bible teaches the concept of the Trinity. Jesus is God. You believe Jesus to be a god but not equal to God. You even put Lucifer at the same level with Christ. You have watered your Jesus down and I doubt that a watered-down Jesus is a saving Jesus. At least there is enough doubt in my mind that I wouldn't bet my soul on it. And more than that, it makes me feel fear for yours."

"But I love Jesus. He is everything to me."

"Tom, you are in far more danger than I am."

"What do you mean?"

"Well, if the Hindus are right we will both be okay, because any serious seeker will be fine. Do you agree?

"Yes, of course."

"And if Buddhists or any other of the eastern religions are right the same conclusion is true. Serious seekers will be okay. Right?"

"Right!"

"So we can also conclude that if "New-Agers" are correct with reincarnation you'll just go around as many times as it take to get it right. If that's true we will still be okay.

"I'm still with you." He was tracking with me.

"If universalists are right we all end up in heaven no matter what, so we will both be okay."

"Go on."

"If anihilationists are correct and those who are wrong just cease to exist as entities when they die, while those who are right go to heaven, whether we are right or wrong doesn't have that much consequence. Ceasing to exist is not as bad as whatever hell is if it's literal."

"Agreed."

"If religion is a hoax and we all turn to dust when we die it doesn't matter what either of us believed. Still with me?

"Yes."

"In the same way, if your watered-down Jesus is a saving Jesus we are both okay, but if my Jesus is the only way, as he has said, then you are probably not okay. No matter what, I'm in the best-possible position. I'm in if he's real. I'm in as good shape as I can be in if he's not. It's an odds thing. With my soul on the line I want the best odds I can get. So I'm goin' with the Christ of the Bible, not the diminished version presented in the Book of Mormon."

He though about that idea for a while and then asked me what I though about heaven. I said, "Your turn. Tell me what you think."

"We can be as God." He was excited. "As we are, God was. As God is we can become."

"Tom, what was original sin?" I asked.

"Adam and Eve disobeying God."

"No, go back further. When was the first created being disobedient to God."

"What are you getting at?" he asked.

"The first time any entity created by God said 'No' to him was when satan wanted to set his throne above the throne of God. 'I will make myself like the most High' is what he said.[58] Now it seems to me that you have gone through the mental gymnastics of justifying what satan got cast out of heaven for trying. You want to become like God and I'm afraid for you. I think you are playing some very long odds adding to the Bible with your other books and I think it's really dangerous to take the words of people and give them equal status with the Bible as you have with your modern-day prophets." My voice was passionate and my eyes had filled with moisture. "My friend, I believe you have made a bad bet."

He was without words for a few moments and then said, "I'll have to think about that. It's something I've never considered before." Then he added, "One of us is wrong."

"For sure," I responded. "But if I'm wrong I'm still okay. If you're wrong you will be in hell. I'm safe. You're not."

I had made my point. But reason didn't convince Tom. And his failure to respond to reason makes Pascal's argument timely.

Pascal's Point (the Wager)

I'm now resorting to the classics. I think it's time to lay an oldie, moldy heavyweight thought on you from one of the world's greatest thinkers. That will tell you how desperate I am over the condition of your soul and your need to trust Christ.

Blaise Pascal said, "Let us examine the point and say: 'Either God exists, or he does not.' But which of the alternatives shall we choose? Reason cannot decide anything."[59] His conclusion is based on our inability to absolutely prove either position. All the reasons in the world won't prove that God exists or that the Bible is real or that Jesus Christ really did die for our sins. But neither will reason disprove those concepts.

Pascal does agree that we have to bet on one or the other. (We can choose not to bet. But then, no bet is still a bet . . . so he's right.) His thinking is, bet God exists because, "If you win you win everything, but if you lose you lose nothing. Don't hesitate, then, but take a bet that he exists."[60] His thinking is that if God doesn't exist, it costs us nothing if we bet that he does.

So far so good, but Pascal fails to talk about the reverse thought—that of betting he doesn't exist if he in fact does. That's a major oversight in his reasoning. Hell is never an issue with him. However, his next thought is a blockbuster. So I choose to finish this book with this thought just in case you have yet to believe in Jesus Christ as your personal Savior. Pascal concludes that reason will never solve your problem:

> But at least you can realize that if you are unable to believe, it is not because of reason, but because of your emotions. So try not to convince yourself by multiplying reasons for God's existence, but by controlling your emotions. You want to have faith, but you do not know the way. You want to be cured of unbelief, and so you ask for the remedy. Learn then from the examples of those who, like yourself, were once in bondage but who now are prepared to risk their whole life. These are those who know the way you would like to follow, and who have been cured of a sickness that you wish also to be healed from. Follow the way by which they began. They simply behaved as though they believed. That

will incline you naturally to accept and to have peace.

'But that's what I'm afraid of!'

But why? What have you to lose? In order to prove to you that it really works, it will control the emotions which for you are such a great stumbling block.

Now what harm will come to you by choosing this course of action? You will be faithful, honest, humble, grateful, full of good works, a sure and gen-uine friend. In fact, you will no longer find yourself swamped by poisonous pleasures, such as those of lust and desire for fame. But won't you have anything else? I assure you that you will gain in this life, and that with every step you take along this way, you will realize you have bet on something sure and infinite which has cost you nothing.

There you have it. With what God gives you in peace and joy in this life and heaven later, you really have nothing to lose by trusting Christ. But you have everything to lose if you don't. Maybe you ought to look through the prayers at the end of chap-ter nine again or at least consider my chance encounter with the Vietnam Memorial.

Memories and Monuments

I had walked from the Capitol Building, past the Washington Monument, to the Lincoln Memorial. It took a little over an hour. I had been in Washington, D.C. doing a Focus on the Family basketball camp . The museums were on my left. Ponds and ducks were off to the right. There were joggers, rollerbladers, walkers, sitters, lovers . . . and lots of tourists. I was just an observer. I never have been much of a tourist. I'm the guy who drove all the way to the Grand Canyon, walked over, took a look and was ready to leave.

After leaving a dignified Mr. Lincoln sitting and staring

endlessly, I took a turn and accidentally came upon the Vietnam Memorial. Suddenly I was no longer a passive observer. There was too much pain to walk by and remain unaffected. Only the hardest of hearts could do that.

"Dear God, he was only seventeen," cried one mom with an inflection in her voice that quietly screamed the depth of her loss.

"Why?" came an angry demand from a dad as he stared at a name etched in the wall.

"Oh how I miss him," wailed a lonely mother, as she clung to her mother. Both were crying.

A dad stood in silence with sobbing daughters under both arms. His chest heaved as he fought his feelings, but the tears chasing down his cheeks showed that he'd failed in his fight for control. He had lost a son . . . he had earned his right to cry.

Brothers and sisters were there too. Some cried openly. Others just whimpered. Many lacked the understanding of the magnitude of what had happened and just stared. But none played. Not even the little ones. The Wall wasn't for fun. Memories of death lingered here.

People were rubbing pencils over paper stretched across an etched name of a loved one, as a kid traces the outline of a coin or a detective discovers the words on the removed top sheet of a notepad by lightly rubbing a pencil over the sheet beneath it. They would take their name home and frame it.

The Memorial had a cleansing effect of finality for some. I watched a few people let go of their anger. Some would never let go. But even those who had let go had been scarred for life. They all had been damaged. Their loved ones were gone.

I never lost a loved one in Nam, but as I left the memorial that summer day I too had been scarred. I don't think I have ever felt anything like that before. I did cry at the Air Force Academy during full dress retreat when the national anthem and taps were played as the colors were struck. Desert Storm had been in full bloom at the time. The experience moved me deeply. And I did cry at the Arizona Memorial in Hawaii. People who pay high prices for God and country do touch me. They are worth crying for. But here, along the black, etched marble, name-stained walls, there was pain that overwhelmed loss. Such pain. I don't think I'll be the same.

I sensed pain in a new way that day in D.C. As a result, I have a little more empathy for folks who hurt. And I think my experience gave me a bit more of an understanding of what our rebellion must do to God. It must hurt him so much. Anyone who loves perfectly also has to hurt perfectly.

But I can't imagine the depth of grief of a God whose creation has turned its back on him. I can't grasp the magnitude of the sins of all humanity being dumped on the shoulders of a single Person. Nor can I imagine that Person accepting the load knowing he'd be rejected by the very ones he did it for. That's too much pain for this guy to comprehend.

Knowing we would kill him, God loved (and loves) us so much that he started the ball rolling anyway . . . almost two thousand years ago in a little town in the Middle East that was then the center of the known world. And he did it knowing that thirty-three years later a grim Friday would have to be endured. It was a Friday when the Romans literally hung him out to dry, after playing "shish-kabob" with his body. But it wasn't the first time he'd been hung out to dry. Judas had done it. So had the rest of the disciples. And it wouldn't be the last. Most of humanity would do the same. Such pain.

I think God took a pencil and rubbed it over a piece of paper stretched across a name etched on a black marble wall that day. It was the name at the top . . . the Name that is above all names. And then I think he cried. What else was there for a Father to do.

But God didn't frame the name. He put it in a Book and gave it to us so that we might remember that there are three days that go together—Christmas, Good Friday and Easter. We must not think of one without considering the other two.

Christmas is the day of beginnings. The journey down the road to the Cross was begun. It's a fun day. Easter is the victory day, of course. And it's a great story. But although the enemy was defeated when death was whipped, Friday had left its awful marks. Christ was still scarred. And not just his wrists and side. In a sense he took the burden of our sin into the timelessness of eternity. A burden he chose to carry forever.

Those of us who accept God's gift are committed to taking the inevitable scars that will come as we conform to the image of his Son and are fitted for service. After all, we have to go through what we go through to help other people get through what we went through. How else could we serve?

But in exchange for the scars loving Jesus brings, our names will be etched on a wall of life, not death. And nobody will cry when they read them. As a matter of fact, everyone who sees them will rejoice—including God, who has already cried and grieved over our sins, and Jesus, who bore them so that our names might be etched on the wall—right next to his.

Put your name in The Book of Life. Play the odds.

Eternity's your bet. Bet on Christ.

Personal Note

If God has used this book to make a difference in your life, drop me a note. It would be an encouragement.

I also have a monthly newsletter. My speaking schedule is always included so you'll know if I'm ever in your area. Indicate on your note if you'd like to receive *Obedient Thoughts*.

If you are interested in audio tapes of this series or other messages I've done let me know. Do the same for any of my books you can't find in your local bookstore. I'll send you a price list so you can order what you want.

Finally, if you need a speaker for your church or a conference write or call:

Jay Carty
Yes Ministries
1735 NW Arthur Circle
Corvallis, OR 97330
(503) 754-7547

Other items by Jay Carty include:

Playing the Odds Audio Cassette Tapes

Counterattack:
Taking Back Ground Lost To Sin

A practical guide to spiritual warfare. Includes a study guide. (Multnomah Press)

Counterattack Video

Five and a half hours of Jay presenting the material from his book *Counterattack*. Consists of seven messages in forty-three to forty-eight minute segments. Audio also available.

Something's Fishy:
Getting Rid of the Carp in Your Life

A book for those who are lukewarm in their faith. (Yes Ministries)

Developing Your Natural Talents
How To Do What You Love and Love What You Do

A guide leading you to the discovery of your God-given natural talents and how to negotiate their use into work and ministry. (NavPress) Study video also available.

Only Tens Go To Heaven

A booklet (30 pages) presenting the gospel message (including repentance) in words and cartoons. It's perfect for the guest bathroom. There are about ten minutes' worth of reading. (Yes Ministries)

Sports Shorts

A collection of 366 athletic quotations in a daily calendar format with three or four spiritual ones per month. A subtle presentation of the gospel in a year. (Garborgs)

WHAT ABOUT THE ONE WHO NEVER HEARD?

(The most often-asked question by those wanting to understand God.)

I led a Bible study for men who are relatively new to the Bible for seven years. Most of us used the same version so we could call out page numbers. It made it easier to turn to the passages we were studying. Men don't like to be embarrassed.

It was the kind of group where you can bring a friend and ask any question any time. Without exception, every man who was new to the Bible and the claims of Christ inquired about the same issue. And each man usually asked his question as if it was the first time anybody ever did, "What happens to the person who never hears—like the guy in the jungle, the tribe on an island, or the one raised in a country where Christianity isn't the mainstream religion? How can God send that person to hell? It just wouldn't be fair."

By now you know most of the answer. Onions and baseball explain a good deal of it, but not all. A deeper understanding of what's involved comes from God's instinctive, progressive and "one-way" revelations. This gets a little theological. That's why this section is in the Appendix.

God's Instinctive Revelation

We'll start with Psalm 19. It contains the first half of God's instinctive revelation:

> The heavens declare the glory of God; the skies proclaim the work of his hands. Day after day they pour forth speech; night after night they display knowledge. There is no speech or language where their voice is not heard. (Psalms 19:1–3)

Go outside and look around. Not at what we have made, but rather, look at the things God has made. And don't make the mistake of looking at those parts of God's creation we have messed up. Study the result of his handiwork, not ours. Then listen.

You won't hear any words. But keep listening anyhow. A sunset screams of God. The Yosemite Valley is the signature of God on the perfect canvas of creation. The Grand Canyon is his doodle during a phone conversation with Christ. Look up at the stars and tell me there is no God. You can't keep from laughing at the absurdity of the thought.

But no, I haven't heard God's voice. There is no speech, nor are there words; his voice is not heard. But it is felt and sensed. No rational person can deny that what we see is the handiwork of God. It's part of God's instinctive revelation—his attempt to show himself to us by planting awareness in our hearts.

That makes it a lot of work to be an atheist. You have to have the Walkman of the world cranked, amped, and plugged into your ears to become deaf enough not to hear. But it can be done. There are more than a few folks who try to ignore God and explain away what he has done.

Psalm 19 is only half of God's instinctive revelation. Romans 1 is the other half. It tells us why so many ignore the essence of the nineteenth Psalm:

> The wrath of God is being revealed from heaven against all the godlessness and wickedness of men who suppress the truth by their wickedness, *since what may be known about God is plain to them, because God*

has made it plain to them. For since the creation of the world God's invisible qualities—his eternal power and divine nature—have been clearly seen, being understood from what has been made, *so that men are without excuse*.

For although they knew God, they neither glorified him as God nor gave thanks to him, but their thinking became futile and their foolish hearts were darkened. Although they claimed to be wise, they became fools and exchanged the glory of the immortal God for images made to look like mortal man and birds and animals and reptiles.

Therefore God gave them over in the sinful desires of their hearts to sexual impurity for the degrading of their bodies with one another. *They exchanged the truth of God for a lie, and worshipped and served created things rather than the Creator*—who is forever praised. Amen. (Romans 1:18–25)

The study of mankind has never revealed a society that doesn't worship. All of the remote tribes in both hemispheres have been found to reverence gods and idols. Every culture in antiquity honored deities. It is true of communities today. We are worshiping critters. God made it so.

The heavens speak because way down, deep inside our souls, God has made himself known to us. God has revealed himself so that on judgment day we won't be able to stand before him and say, "But I didn't know!"

Romans 1:22 tells us that most of mankind has claimed their own wisdom and have declared no need of God. They have become fools by worshiping themselves or things they have made, such as idols and trumped-up deities.

> Most won't worship the true God,
> but they can't get away from worship.

God has created an empty space inside of each person that can only be filled with himself, no matter how hard we try to fill it with other things or ourselves. In other words, it takes a lot of work to be an atheist. Not only do people have to ignore what God has done around them, they have to silence his still small voice inside them. But that can be done. Many in Soviet leadership did it.

Ron Carlson, the internationally known authority on cults, was speaking about the funeral of a Russian leader a few years ago. The body was being viewed. The proceedings were cold and atheistic. It was then that Chernenko's wife threw herself across his body and made the sign of a cross.[61] You can take a wife out of the church, but it's hard to take the church out of the wife. It's hard to be an atheist. His wife wasn't and she sure didn't want her husband in hell. But her gesture didn't change a thing.

God has demonstrated himself to all peoples of all ages through instinctive revelation. If people respond to the awareness of God within them, it is up to God to show more. If they don't respond to instinctive revelation, there is no need to show them more light. But if they do, he will amplify the revelation of himself. I call it his progressive revelation.

God's Progressive Revelation

J. Robertson Mcquilkin put it this way:

> I'd like to suggest that God's judgment is based on man's response to light received. We do not believe that men are lost for not believing in Christ when they have never heard of Christ. They are lost when they do not receive and act upon the light they have. In Luke 12:47 we read of the end time, the

judgment day, when the righteousness or unrighteousness of God must stand forth, 'That servant who
knows his master's will and does not get ready or does
not do what his master wants will be beaten with
many blows.'

The gracious girl in Japan who, brought up in
the Buddhist tradition, has been a good daughter and
a good wife and giving to her children but has never
heard of Christ is not in the same condition as the
American who can turn on the television or the radio
to hear the gospel any day of the week, who passes
church after church on the way to the bar, but who
continually rejects the light.

Continuing Luke 12:48, 'But the one who does
not know and does things deserving punishment will
be beaten with few blows. From everyone who has
been given much, much will be demanded; and from
the one who has been entrusted with much, much
more will be asked.'

What is God's response to those who do receive
the light? God's response to obedience is always more
light.[62]

For those who respond, God will also progressively respond.
God has set eternity in the hearts of men (Ecclesiastes 3:11).
Man continues to reach out for God. And God has not left himself without testimony (Acts 14:16–17). Those who want to find
him can. He will continually reveal himself to those who seek.

Don Richardson has written several books about the amazing biblical parallels among tribes and cultures around the world.
These are evidences of God's progressive revelation. He cites
tribes that have made reference to the one "genuine" God with
names for him that are similar to Hebrew, only there was no way
they could have ever been exposed to Hebrew.[63] Others awaited a
lost Book that would tell them about "The God" that was to be
brought to them by people outside their tribe, and some of these

tribes are on different continents.[64] Some tribes, whose people had never been exposed to Christianity, even had "Christian" symbols incorporated in their languages. For example, the Chinese symbol for righteous is a lamb with the letter "I" under it, meaning—I under the lamb am righteous! The ideograph denoting a tree is a cross with the symbol for man superimposed upon it![65] This is just a small sample of three volumes of evidence Richardson has compiled.

God has been showing himself to the people of the world for a long time. From Adam, to Abraham, to today. And what he has revealed has been consistent. As a matter of fact, Richardson has observed a seven-component pattern in the revelations:

> (1) the fact of God's existence; (2) creation; (3) the rebellion and fall of man; (4) the need for a sacrifice to appease God and the crafty attempts of devils to make men sacrifice to them; (5) the great Flood; (6) the sudden appearance of many languages and the resulting dispersion of mankind into many peoples; and finally (7) an acknowledgment of man's need of some further revelation that will seal man back into a blessed relationship with God.
>
> These seven major facts which were known before Abraham's time are still included—in a declining order of statistical occurrence—among the main components of folk religions worldwide. The degree to which any folk religion has maintained its hold on truth can be measured by how many of these seven components it still retains and with what clarity.[66]

If tribes around the world have these common components in their cultures, don't we have to conclude that God has been showing himself? I think so. The common thread is more like a huge anchor chain. If you look, you can't miss the connection. And those who respond will get even more light. But those who don't, won't. And for them the progressive revelation of light will stop.

But what about those who keep responding? God gets real specific.

The "One-Way" Revelation

What about other sacred books; what about those who believe the Koran instead of the Bible? What about other religions with followers outnumbering those following Christ? What about eastern beliefs? What about native Americans? What about . . . ? It depends on whether the whole deal is real. Basically, it depends on God's "one-way" revelation.

Jesus Christ made a statement that, if true, makes all the rest of the world's religions wrong. He does it with the "one-way" verse, "I am the way and the truth and the life. No one comes to the Father except through me" (John 14:6). In other words, if you want to get to God the Father you have to go through the Son. If you want to go where God is when your physical life is over, you'll have to go through Christ. No other way will work. Jesus also made it clear, if you want to know the Father you have to know the Son, and if you don't know One you don't know the Other (John 14:7–11).

My conclusion regarding the nice people who are on the earth today is that God will get someone to them to tell them about Jesus if they respond to both God's instinctive and progressive revelations. It happened in the past with an Ethiopian in a chariot. God sent Philip to explain the Bible to the man (Acts 8:26–39). God will follow-up on his "one-way" revelation today just as he did then. This book may be his method with you.

But the prime question remains unanswered. There were people alive right after Christ died who wouldn't have had the opportunity to hear the name of Christ. What about them? And what about those people in remote areas of the world today where missionaries have yet to penetrate. We still haven't resolved what happens to them. What happens if you don't get the Good News about Jesus Christ? What if no one brings you the message? What happens to those who might respond if they were told?

What About the Person Who Would Receive but Never Hears?

"Abram believed the Lord, and he credited it to him as righteousness." (Genesis 15:6) In the Old Testament, although the final sacrifice hadn't yet been provided for sin, if you believed God, you would not go to hell. As I said, the animal sacrifices performed on your behalf were a "Sinterest only" payment of sorts on your debt until Christ paid off the balance on the Cross.

The word "believe" in that passage means more than intellectual agreement. It connotes coming alongside of God, alignment, commitment, and repentance. Proper biblical belief requires a change of heart. Abram had a heart for God.

In the Old Testament, the righteous (the ones who believed properly) who died went to upper Hades and awaited the event on the Cross. Jesus came and took them to heaven.

How many believed God that way? Who knows? The folks of faith mentioned in the faith chapter (Hebrews 11) did. They are examples of those Old Testament righteous who believed correctly.

The chapter starts off with a definition of faith[67]

> Now faith is the assurance of things hoped for,
> the conviction of things not seen . . .

That is followed by a statement regarding the Old Testament faithful:

> For by it the men of old gained approval.

God then tells us that if you don't think he is behind the creation of the world, you might not have enough faith to get saved:

"By faith we understand that the worlds were prepared by the word of God, so that what is seen was not made out of things which are visible."

There is a listing of the Old Testament super stars of faith—some of the men, plus a lady, who believed God and were counted as righteous. The list includes Abel, Enoch, Noah, Abraham, Isaac, Jacob, Joseph, Moses, Rahab, Gideon, Samson, Jephthah, David, Samuel and the prophets.

Finally, at the end of the chapter there is a statement confirming the necessity of the event of the Cross:

> These were all commended for their faith, *yet none of them received what had been promised*. God had planned something better for us so that only together with us would they be made perfect. (Hebrews 12:1–40)

In other words, the Old Testament righteous had to wait for Christ to die on the Cross before they could get out of Hades and into heaven. But even though they hadn't heard the name of Jesus Christ they were ultimately saved by his name.

Think It Through

Do you think there might have been a person of faith living somewhere on the earth the day before Christ was crucified? Sure! Maybe.

How about on the day Christ died? Yeah! If there was one living the day before, it is likely that the person would still be alive one day later.

How about the day after? If you said "yes" to the first two questions, you have to say "yes" to this one. But do the old rules apply even though God made a new deal when Christ did away with the law and swapped it with grace?

There certainly hadn't been enough time to get the word out yet. And even while Jesus was walking around, John the

Baptist was baptizing with the baptism of repentance. That's just another way of saying they believed God and it was still counted to them as righteousness. John's disciples were like Abraham.

What about one baptized by John who died before finding out about Jesus' death? Answer: Old Testament rules applied to those who hadn't heard. If you believed God properly you were counted as righteous.

The Ten Commandments weren't given as mandates for us to keep. They were given to show how far we are from God's holiness—proof that we're onions. That's why God's commandments aren't difficult to keep . . . they're impossible.

Even though the law dominates, grace is found in the Old Testament. Remember, animal sacrifices temporarily paid the interest on our debt (sin), until Christ paid off the balance (grace). If you believed during Old Testament times, God's grace preserved your soul until Christ paid your debt.

When Christ died, grace presided over the law, but Old Testament rules still applied to those who hadn't heard. If that was true for the disciples of John the Baptist, the same rules must also apply to those who haven't heard about Jesus today.[68]

Jesus said he is the only way into the Kingdom. Are there exceptions? I don't know for sure, but I think so.

It's appointed for a person to die once and then comes the judgment. Are there exceptions? Sure! Enoch and Elijah never died. Lazarus, Jarius' daughter, the widow's son, the girl Peter raised, and the boy Elijah raised from the dead all had to die twice. The disciples raised some, too. So God is perfectly capable of making exceptions to his rules. But before we get too carried away with the "Golden Rule," think about this.

The scholars agree that there were at least several million people alive on the earth in the days of Noah. I don't know how many million, but living to the ages they did gave them lots of time to make lots and lots of kids. And they kept making them—

for hundreds and hundreds of years. I'll bet they took populating the earth seriously.

Of all those millions of people, how many believed God? Take a guess. We know for sure. The Bible tells us.

Just one! Noah (Genesis 6:5-9). And because of him, God let his wife and his sons and their wives live. But not because of their righteousness—just because of Noah's. And he wasn't all that righteous. He just believed God. It's important to understand the significance of this point because of the next question.

How many people do you think there are out there today who haven't heard the good news about Jesus Christ, who believe God the way Abraham, Noah and John the Baptist's disciples did?

I don't know either. But if the hearts of those in our world bear any resemblance to the hearts of Noah's contemporaries, there aren't many. In that day there was only Noah. There may not be any today.

Mcquilkin's conclusion to the question about those who haven't heard may sound like a cop-out but I rather like it:

> Suppose you and I were the safety officers on the tenth floor of a condominium which cared for elderly patients. Fire broke out. We, having done our job well, knew that the official floor plan posted on the wall identified one fire escape at the end of the corridor. Perhaps it would be legitimate for me to turn over in my mind the idea that surely the architect must have put in another fire escape. Then, too, I remembered reading a newspaper story of someone who fell out of a tenth floor apartment and landed in a bush and survived. It might be all right for me to think of that. I'm not sure. It might be all right for me to think of tying sheets together so that some unusually strong octogenarian could climb down. But I

think it would be immoral to propose such ideas in an hour like that. What do you think?

I may not be able to prove from Scripture that no one since Calvary has ever reached heaven without a knowledge of Jesus Christ. But neither can it be proved from Scripture that anyone has done so. If it were true that people could be saved in other ways, and if it were good for people to know that, would not the Bible have told us so? Since it does not give us this hope, the hope must either be false or it must be good for people not to know about it. In either event, it would be wrong for me to speculate and propagate such an idea, because the Bible does not do so, and if it proves a false hope, what damage it would have done![69]

A story has been told about a missionary walking through the jungle who meets a man.[70] They pause on the trail to get acquainted. The man asks why the missionary has come, so the missionary tells the man about Jesus Christ.

The next words out of the native's mouth are a show stopper, "So that's his name!" He continued speaking, "I stopped worshiping my tribe's gods to worship the three-in-one God that was revealed to me. I was to do it through the Son of that God. And until today I never knew his name. I have been persecuted greatly by my people, but I have been faithful in my worship." It appears that the man believed God, and I'll bet it was counted to him as righteousness before he heard about Christ. If the missionary never showed, I believe the man would have been counted like Abraham. But remember, I don't know for sure.

Can you follow the teachings of religions devised by man and be righteous? I think the first chapter of Romans says no, but what do I know? How about a long reluctant "perhaps!" Can you never hear the name of Jesus Christ and be saved? I think it's possible. But there won't be very many others—if any at all. Remember how many there weren't in Noah's day.

The Struggle

What about Buddhists, Hindus, and nice people in other religions who haven't heard? What about them? Dear friend, they are onions like you and me, but I think they will be judged by Old Testament law. And that's a whole lot tougher than New Testament grace. By Old Testament law you have to bat a thousand. Under New Testament grace you have to be on the right team. Which is easier to do?

Regardless of what happens to those who haven't heard, I trust my loving God to be fair. Actually, that's what I'm afraid of. I don't want him to be fair. They'll get justice if he is. I want him to be more than merciful, too. I want them to have eternal life, not just more time. What I really want is for God to extend grace to them. But he can't do that and be fair unless it's through Jesus Christ. So I pray for exceptions.

After all this dialogue we're still not sure what happens to the person who never hears. But what happens won't make any difference to you. You have heard. And not dealing with Christ because you don't know what's going to happen to someone else is a smoke screen. Basically, it's a cop out. You're skirting the real issue. Don't bail on me now. If you didn't decide in previous chapters, what are you going to do with Jesus Christ?

Who Do You Say That He Is?

God sent Christ to communicate the depth of his love for us and to show how far away from God we have gone. Jesus is the only solution to the problem of sin (the stuff that separates us from God). God wants us to know about his Son. And once he has shown Christ to you, the next move is yours.

God's "one-way" revelation requires a response. Remember what Peter said. he had the right answer:

> Once when Jesus was praying in private and his disciples were with him, he asked them, 'Who do the crowds say I am?'

They replied, 'Some say John the Baptist; others say Elijah; and still others, that one of the prophets of long ago has come back to life.'

'But what about you?' he asked. 'Who do you say I am?'

Peter answered, *'The Christ of God.'* (John 9:18–20)

There are a lot of things being said about Jesus Christ. In some circles he is a swear word. In New-Age circles he's anything, anyone, and everywhere. In public schools he's a "no-no." But God is not concerned with groups. He wants individual relationships.

"What about you? Who do you say that he is?"

Peter's answer was the equivalent of "my personal Savior." He had responded properly to God's "one way" revelation.

God has obviously given you his instinctive revelation. You must have responded because he has shown you his progressive revelation. You must have responded because this book is his "one-way" revelation for you. If you respond to it you'll become a child of God.

Eternity's still your choice.

1   I've heard, but not confirmed, that 90 percent of all decisions for Christ occur by the age of twenty-five and that 85 percent are made before leaving high school.

2   People Magazine, 12 June 1978.

3   Original source unknown. I received the quote from my friend John Lotz, who is the Assistant Athletic Director, University of North Carolina.

4   "The heart is more deceitful than all else and is desperately sick; Who can understand it?" (Jeremiah 17:9)

5   "And there is salvation in no one else; for there is no other name under heaven that has been given among men, by which we must be saved" (Acts 4:12).

6   Jesus said to him, "I am the way, and the truth, and the life; no one comes to the Father, but through Me. (John 14:6)

7   Pratney, Winkie. The Holy Bible—Wholly True. (Pretty Good Printing: Lindale, Texas, 1979).

8   MacArthur, John F. Jr., Why Believe the Bible. (Regal Book: Glendale, Calif., 1978) 41.

9   Ibid., 52.

10   Ibid., 57

11   MacArthur

12   McDowell & Stewart. Reasons Skeptics Should Consider Christianity, 76

13   McDowell, Josh. Evidence That Demands A Verdict. (Here's Life Publishers, Inc.: San Bernardino, California) 39–40.

14   McDowell & Stewart. Reasons Skeptics Should Consider Christianity, 75

15   Josh McDowell and Don Stewart. Answers to Tough Questions. (Tyndale House Publishers, Inc.: Wheaton, Illinois) 35.

16   McDowell. Evidence That Demands a Verdict., 144–166. This is the best listing of which I am aware and is must reading.

17   Ibid., 167.

18   Ibid., 167.

19   MacArthur, 9.

20   McDowell & Stewart. Reasons Skeptics Should Consider Christianity, 74-75

21   Billy Graham, "The Authority of Scripture." Decision (June 1963).

22   Gallup, 60

23   Ibid., 60

24   Ibid., 60

25 Ibid., 60

26 James Patterson and Peter Kim. *The Day America Told the Truth* (New York: Prentice Hall Press, 1991), 25–26

27 "What a Life Is Worth: U.S. Seeks a Price." *U.S. News & World Report*, 16 September 1985, 58

28 Ibid

29 Ibid

30 Ibid

31 Carlson message, 7 July 1991.

32 Billy Graham, *Facing Death*. (Word Books: Waco,Texas,1987) 57

33 Tony Campolo. "Christian Camping in the '90s." Tape. Hume Lake Christian Camps. 1991.

34 Sloat, Donald E., *The Dangers of Growing Up in a Christian Home*. (Thomas Nelson, Inc.: Nashville, Tennessee) 112

35 John H. Gerstner. *Repent or Perish*. (Soli Deo Gloria Publications: Ligonier, Pennsylvania) 13

36 Ibid., 23

37 Ibid., 28

38 George Gallup, Jr. and Jim Castelli. *The People's Religion*. (MacMillan Publishing Company: New York) 45–59

39 Graham, 36

40 John Stott. *Evangelical Essentials*; Philip Hughes, *The True Image*; Edward William Fudge. *The Fire That Consumes*; and others.

41 John H. Gerstner. *Repent or Perish* (Soli Deo Gloria Publications: Lignier, Pennsylvania) 29.

42 Billy Graham, *Facing Death*. (Word Books: Waco, Texas, 1987) 34

43 *The Zondervan Pictorial Bible Dictionary* (Zondervan Publishing House: Grand Rapids, Michigan, 1963) 956

44 Chafer. 429

45 Although their opinion is in the vast minority, a few commentators do not believe the compartment theory is correct. Some believe the Old Testament saints went straight to heaven. Moses and Elijah being with Christ at the Transfiguration suggest they were in heaven not Hades. And Christ told the thief on the cross next to him that they would be in paradise that very day, not Hades. The argument is academic. Moses and Elijah could have come from the penthouse and Christ could have done his thing in Hades before the thief died. It doesn't matter who is correct since we all agree that those who die in Christ today are in heaven.

46 LaHaye, Tim. *How to Study Bible Prophecy for Yourself.* (Harvest House Publishers: Eugene, Oregon) 181

47 Ibid., 184

48 Ibid., 185

49 Kennedy, 75

50 Tenney, Merrill C., Gen Ed. *The Zondervan Pictorial Bible Dictionary.* 497

51 MacArthur, John. Tape series. "Heaven." The Master's Communication. P.O. Box 4000, Panorama City, Calif. 91412, 1987. (Note—My thanks to Dr. MacArthur. This series was terrific. I relied on it heavily in the writing of this chapter.)

52 Ibid. (The quotation is not exact. I transcribed it from the tape and adapted it for copy.)

53 Kennedy, 66

54 Watterson, Calvin and Hobbes. Newspaper Syndication. 23 December 1990

55 Chafer, Lewis Sperry, *Systematic Theology.* (Dallas Seminary Press: Dallas, Texas, vol. IV) 430

56 Remember, this is the big-time Apostle Paul who is struggling. So you will probably struggle, too.

57 If we confess our sins, he is faithful and just and will forgive us our sins and purify us from all unrighteousness.

58 "But you said in your heart, 'I will ascend to heaven; I will raise my throne above the stars of God, And I will sit on the mount of assembly In the recesses of the north. I will ascend above the heights of the clouds; I will make myself like the Most High.' " (Is. 14:13–14)

59 Pascal, Blaise. *The Mind on Fire.* (Multnomah Press: Portland, Oregon, 1989) 130–131.

60 Ibid.,131.

61 Ron Carlson was speaking at Hume Lake Christian Camps on 7 July 1991.

62 McQuilkin, J. Robertson. *The Narrow Way,* 131.

63 Richardson, Don. *Eternity in Their Hearts.* (Regal Books: Ventura, California, 1978) 9–71.

64 Ibid.,73–109.

65 Ibid.,128–129.

66 Ibid.,155–156

67 I like the New American Standard version for this passage.

68 Some believe that the baptism of repentance applied for the generation of which John was a part and ended thereafter. It is not a strong argument bib-

lically.

69 McQuilkin, 133–134

70 I do not have a source for the story and am not sure it's true. Someone thought it was from a Wycliffe publication. Another thought it came from one of Don Richardson's books. I couldn't find it in either. But it doesn't matter. It still illustrates what God is capable of doing if he chooses.